Praise

"Personal, charming, and endearing. As a fellow Jersey girl with sensory issues, Parsons' writing hits right to the core, conjuring smells of grandma's kitchen and summoning the feeling of scratchy shag carpet on a hot summer's day. Her storytelling language is sensual and visceral, holding space for the not often articulated for people with extrasensory perception. Her work offers us permission to take up as much space as we need and encourages us through her example to allow ourselves as many accommodations as we need to feel human."

JOCELYN MACKENZIE, RECORDING ARTIST,
RIGHTEOUS BABE RECORDS

"Reading Elaina Battista-Parsons' memoir, *Chomp, Press, Pull,* is a fully immersive experience. A rapture of memory pieces filtered through the lens of an artist neurologically more alive to her experience of the senses than most. This beautifully rendered collection of essays refract her life from a perspective that grabs you by the heart and pulls you in chin deep. A tour de force from the author of *Italian Bones in the Snow*, this book is a joy delivery system."

CAROLYN RUSSELL, AUTHOR OF
DEATH AND OTHER SURVIVAL STRATEGIES

About the Author

Elaina is a published author: *Italian Bones in the Snow, Black Licorice,* and *Heart and Salt.* She loves her family, New Jersey downtowns, ice cream, her dog, music, and reading. She wants you to be brave and do the uncomfortable things. Elaina fights for LGBTQ+ rights as a fierce ally. She's currently enrolled in a graduate program (Museum Studies) through CUNY. She's currently working on a picture book about motherhood, but with a twist.

elainawrites.com

CHOMP PRESS PULL

Elaina Battista-Parsons

Chomp, Press, Pull

Print Edition
ISBN: 978-3-98832-143-5
Published by Vine Leaves Press 2025

Cover design by Jessica Bell
Interior design by Amie McCracken

For Uncle Tony.

8/2/62 to 9/17/23

We celebrate you and miss you all the time.

Author's Note

For those individuals with sensory issues who grew up during a time when not much was spoken about, you probably did the best you could. I do not claim to be an expert, nor a scientist. Just a girl who needs her environment a little more regulated in order to function. I remember the events to the very best of my knowledge. Mostly I want you to laugh.

Introduction

In the winter of 1995, my backbone sank into the metal chair in Mrs. Grill's high school AP English class as I choked on a headache the size of Madison Square Garden. I was in no mood to explain the nuances of Jack London's boring voice. Examples? Evidence? I couldn't. The heat pumped through the midcentury-HVAC system, and I was its target, fading fast from the inappropriate warmth. Writing with clarity was an impossible scenario for a teenager who was always hot, naturally. The air shot out of that clunky cage, invisible balloons of pressure that climbed, then climaxed in a nerve-ending frenzy. In this case, my sinuses imploded through the tunnels of my head, acid drizzled toward my stomach, inducing a vomit-on-the-way.

I knew enough to stand up and skid into the hallway where the air was much colder and fresh, and where I couldn't smell AJ Martin's breath from two feet away. In heat, breaths ripen. Sharp, oozy, and in this instance, not creamsicle-like. When breaths smell, even the tiniest bit (not in the creamsicle family), an almost seventeen-year-old like me was sent over the edge and straight into a remote area like the end of hallway. I had to accept my academic fate with this exam. None of my peers noticed that I darted from my seat. *Nerds.*

I grew up ultra-aware of my senses in a way that felt and feels … hectic. But also, divine. The sensory stuff doesn't budge or disappear after childhood, so it must be acknowledged, then managed. It's a sensory regulation and dysregulation thing. My therapist is in the school of pushing into a feeling, rather than running from it with Band-Aid breathing and "positive vibes" only. In other words, the best way to deal with things, is to see it, feel it wholly, then refuse to let it ruin your day. It has its moment, so that eventually, it doesn't. Validation, then elimination.

That day in Senior AP English—because of the unbearable temperature in the room that no one else seemed to notice—my essay score suffered, and nothing could be done to retrace my steps.

"Mrs. Grill, can I open a window, please?" I asked after returning to my seat. How could no other classmates feel that swarm of dirty heat radiating up their nostrils?

"Elaina, it's the middle of January."

"Can I work in the hallway?"

"No. That won't work, Elaina. This is an official test."

Then excuse me while I swallow the acid from my esophagus and work through this sinus migraine, all while smelling AJ's chicken parmigiana loaded with garlic from dinner the night before. I can't believe I didn't vomit. I rested my face on the dirty, scribbled-on desk, like I had many times in elementary school, because it was cold. I didn't care for Jack London's drivel, so maybe I deserved it. My test score was high enough to obtain *some* college English class credits, but not high enough for scholarship money. I call: *problem.*

There was also a day in May in the early 2000s when I was supposed to fight Trenton, NJ on behalf of the Manalapan Teachers' Union. Our contracts were up, and there were many contractual bullet points to be argued and negotiated as a team armed with T-Shirts and signs. I had attended every union meeting throughout the fall and winter, retrieved and relayed all the information to teachers in my building. I felt confident about the knowledge and preparation for this contract fight. When the day came to get to the state capitol, the bus exhaust turned on me. I physically exited the bus, but I had nothing left to offer Trenton after that shaky and loud ride up the Jersey turnpike from Manalapan. Sensory sabotage, and for something worth my time, not like Jack London's voice only about a decade before this. I should've driven to Trenton in my own car, separately, but even at twenty-seven years old, I didn't have a full grip on my issues because it wasn't talked about. My issues were cast aside as me being challenging. *Cranky.*

People around me, as a kid, then teen and beyond, must've often found me difficult to be near at times, or perhaps thought I was sort of a Nervous Nelly. Adults often spoke in tones that implied "get over it, kid." Yes, my nervous system was fully responsible, and no, I wasn't doing it on purpose, by any means. I know now that my nervous system was not relaying messages properly. I know now that I was drowning in a zigzag of messages between my brain and my nerves.

Sensory Processing Disorder was first known as Sensory Integration dysfunction, and discussed by occupational therapist, Anna Jean Ayres in 1972. Basically, if your senses affect the productivity of your daily living in a leisure, play, or professional environment, you may get a diagnosis. I've never been diagnosed nor categorized as having a sensory disorder or condition. I'm so happy for those children who've been diagnosed and now have resources. If a child, teen, or young adult requires accommodations and modifications for their sensory processing they will likely receive them. Tools are more accessible than ever, and for that, I celebrate progress. Over the years I've taught and met students who needed to squeeze a stress ball, push on the wall, or twist a gadget. It makes me feel relief for them, especially having been one of them at their age. We now have dialogue about sensory issues, and as a teacher of students with disabilities my heart grows when I hear the din of those conversations.

I really don't want this to be a book about the disorder itself, since I don't have the diagnosis and don't feel qualified enough to even present the research to you. I will save the bulk of the science for scientists and scholars. I'd much rather make you laugh and squirm.

If you're reading this and thinking, *Crap. I went to school with Elaina. Did she think I had bad breath?* Stop worrying. You might have, but I probably did too. We were kids. And if it really stunk, it's likely because you ate something delicious only hours earlier—something drenched in onions and garlic—and for that, I don't judge you.

Sensory stuff is not always easy to manage, but once you learn the triggers you can maneuver your way across social settings in a reasonable way. A way no one will really notice. It's like driving in your dreams, sort of. In my dream the brake and gas pedal are always made of cardboard. The gas pedal is usually hard to reach, and this is all if I can even find my parked car in the first place—you know, in that huge mall parking lot that changes in appearance every time I turn the corner at the JC Penney's. It shrinks and expands every time I complete one revolution around the building. Basically, it's not easy at first, but you learn tricks along the way and become accustomed to the inevitable hiccups of life.

Back to that cold air that I desperately seek in times of sensory strife—the way to kill someone like me to is to put her in a submarine for as little as three hours. Dead. Even though it has the dark and solitude I love, there's no fresh air to stick your face into. Because you know—there isn't fresh air. There's only sea, and there's only the reality of being closed in. Even if I don't open a window, to *know* I can open it makes all the difference. Airplanes are rough. I'm not afraid to fly in the traditional sense. I'm more afraid of suffocation midair. The cabin pressure. The lack of a cool breeze waiting for me somewhere in the vicinity of my face. More accessible, you could kill me by tying me to a chair, turn the thermostat up to seventy-five, light some "clean cotton" candles, and leave me there for a few hours covered in a fleece blanket. Even in the middle of the coldest day of winter. Dead. If you really want to have fun, play some modern country music.

When I was forty-two, I had a surgery that required me to remain in the ICU for twenty-four hours, and you can be sure I asked nicely for a window to be opened. "I'm so sorry. They are locked permanently," was their answer.

"Why?" I asked.

"Because people ... have ... you know ..."

Yeah. I know. I really do.

°

I can't include sound or taste in the categories of senses that make me the worst version of myself because there's nothing truly negative to say. I love you, cold dairy lusciousness called ice cream. Bless your heart, tandoori chicken smothered in yogurt sauce and the brilliant spices of India. Hey lentil soup, are you single? You're lovely. Music with bass, treble, and everything in between—keep it coming, DJ. I can't recall any textural problems with food, and I can't recall being somewhere thinking the noise was spinning me into my own personal cyclone. I have a friend who admitted to me that music with certain sound and qualities can bring her to the brink of throwing up. I haven't experienced that because perhaps my nervous system doesn't view those sounds as a threat to my own balance.

o

I got lost in the original Shoprite of Toms River, NJ in 1984, and it wasn't my mom's fault. It was one of two things: either I was seduced by the Easter Bunny coloring pages on the large window by the register, or I was laser focused on the selection of gumball and prize machines at the front of the store near customer service. Most likely I became fixated on the one with the full globe of bright pink gumballs the size of Ping-Pong balls. I was enamored and still am, by arrays. You know those fruit stands in New York outside of the bodegas? The flowers, oranges, lemons, melons, you name it? I could look at an array all day. Even my own doodles consist of stacks, piles, and rows of anything you can stack, pile, or sort: cookies, gumballs, flowers, marbles, ribbons, rocks, and light garlands. The Easter Bunny coloring pages weren't dissimilar from this, as kids my age who also loved colors filled that page with crayon streaks, either soft like a feather or loud like a drum solo. It all depended on the colorer's crayon press preference. Were you a shade-in with the side of the crayon person, or a give it all you got kind of crayon master? My mom found me thanks to the PA system.

My very first memory of a book is *The Book of Seasons* by Alice and Martin Provensen. Every page is delicious, every stroke of watercolor or acrylics leaves my nervous system calm. There's a particular page where the kids are standing barefoot on a hill.

The colors burst off the page, but in a muted, earthy way. It's spectacular, and the page refreshes my feeling of being alive. I continue in my adult life to seek artifacts, like tarot cards, that resemble this same muted color scheme—one that feels calm to touch because the colors are subdued.

In my thirties I experienced a real wave of kinesthetic pursuit—sewing fabrics by hand to the voice of Billie Holiday in my kitchen. I'd purchase patterned fabric from Joann's by the yard. I sewed symmetrical square gifts for craft shows, friends, and family. It was part nesting ritual, and part "I need to do something with my hands every day while my baby naps so I don't lose my mind."

I learned during this time of my life that if I didn't create things, anything, I developed anxiety in my body and I'd get stuck, both mentally and often physically to the point where I had to get Reiki sessions to get unstuck.

"Elaina. You have to either exercise or make things to stay well." My Reiki therapist changed my life with those words. "You are both a natural athlete and creator, and when you neglect either of those, your body will let you know, like it is right now."

Where and when did all of this begin? My very first memory of being a human being involves a pink and black polka dot birthday hat—the cone shaped paper kind with the paper fringe around the edge, which was also pink. I remember the feeling of the uneven fringe in my fingers. The smell of the vanilla icing on my rectangular birthday cake that my mom made me. It was edged in gumdrops. Neighborhood kids and preschool kids were scattered around our house. I was turning four so it must've been February, and we were in my family room with the blue carpet. Can everyone recall their first memory in terms of their senses? Maybe.

We should talk about the difference between having strong senses of smell and touch and temperature versus having it control your life. Here's an example: if I'm in a movie theater and someone is coughing in a pattern, say every fifteen seconds nonstop, my entire experience is screwed. I can't concentrate on the movie because their cough goes right through me. *Oh, but it's a sound,* and I said sounds don't bug me. This isn't music. This is someone's mucus rattling around in their throat and chest for everyone to hear in a constant pattern. It sends my nervous system to places that are cruel, and it takes every bit of self-control for me remain with my family in that theater.

I've had people tell me that this feeling of mine is insensitive to those with chronic coughs. I have no answers. It's a private, paid-for situation where we all should consider *where* we are and what we will be doing in relation to other attendees? It's not in the middle of a beach or a public park. I feel for the individual with the cough, I really do, but does that mean it's okay for everyone else to not be able to enjoy the physical space?

Only recently, my husband and I were out to eat in New Paltz, New York and a teen girl coughed ferociously every two minutes. A wet cough that needed medical attention. I couldn't eat my meal as she was only about eight feet away. Is it wrong for me to think, "Maybe take a cough drop, drink some tea, or maybe wait until it subsides to go eat in public around others?" I don't know. I wanted to enjoy my meal. The restaurant was crowded, so moving tables wasn't an option.

Now that I know how to manage my sensory environment, life is better. It took years of life, Reiki training, self-awareness, and breathing properly. It also took fresh chunks of ginger root, tabletop fans, sound machines, air purifiers, ice packs, and a husband who rubs my scalp while we watch Netflix. It also requires the occasional visit to the very strong women who offer chair massages in local malls. The strength of their elbows and thumbs makes my life a better one. Also, goddess bless lord and savior Jonathan Van Ness for their perfect breakdown explanation of how indica can help me across the anxiety mountain during the sleepy hours of the night.

Teeth

Teeth marks dotted my childhood. Literally. If there was something to be bitten or gnawed, I was the kid that would find the object, destroy it, one jaw descent, then ascent, at a time. Not out of any malicious motive. It was about instinct and the need to regulate something crooked inside of my chemistry. Maybe I was a wolf in my past life. A lion, tiger, some fierce carnivore that had to keep her babies safe and their stomachs full. My teeth have always been where I lead from, as far back as I remember. Funny enough, I never bit another child.

I take that back. According to my mom, I bit my brother's head when he was only a baby. I'm sure it was out of love, like a mama dog who bites her puppy's scruff and carries him around. I'm making that up. It's likely I bit him because I could or because I was seeking attention from my mom when she brought him home from the hospital.

My mom had this small yellow reused margarine container in which she'd store her sewing pins. The pins stuck together in clumps, and colorful pinheads pointed themselves in every direction. Besides sticking my finger in this mess of thin steel pins for touch-pleasure, my favorite thing to do was to remove the lid of the Tupperware, place it into my little mouth with the lid rim up, and bite down. The plastic lined up with my teeth and gums in a way that provided pressure relief and input. I'd bite down hard, but not hard enough to make it bleed. Just hard enough to gain the relief my nervous system sought. This pastime certainly should've indicated that something was off kilter in my nerve center, but nonetheless, nobody hurt themselves, so I can't blame my parents. It just wasn't a topic or concern to be discussed.

If there was a container of Play-Doh, that cap was coming off with my teeth. If there was a leather chair at my grandma's house, it would not have been complete with a small portion of stuffing oozing out of it, courtesy of my two front teeth. My parents never let me live that one down. Who doesn't love a shiny brown chunk of leather for lunch? I distinctly remember the urge to bite things or to bite down for input. Luckily, I outgrew many of the teeth habits. But not before causing some damage in rooms and cars and toyboxes.

Barbies stood zero chance of survival in my house. Plastic rods shot through every foot after I chomped on their ankles. I chewed their hands and feet with great fervor. *All* of mine were weird Barbies. With an ability of a sculptor, I turned and positioned my teeth like hands and the point chisel. If you gave me a pumpkin at that age, I probably would have won a jack-o-lantern contest. Smurf figurines, necklaces, marker caps—all between my teeth with scars to prove it.

According to my mom, my wooden crib was chewed up from one end to the other, as I opened my mouth, set my teeth between the wooden bars and gnawed. Following this ritual, I jumped up and down for hours. Years later, we rode around my Jersey Shore town daily in my mom's white Buick station wagon with the interior green leather—-that headrest stood no chance either. Pluck, chew. Like a giant pair of tweezers in the shape of baby teeth. My god, the pressure and input I must've required to be able to make those piercings in leather sewn that tight. I did it though, I bit down and through, and the stuffing poking through never got stuffed back in quite the same.

Nail polish was ubiquitous in the average kid's life in the 1980s and '90s. I must have swallowed more dried nail polish flakes than any other person I know. Oh my god, when they'd flake off in a whole piece, it was sensory celebration to the max, like an accomplishment to shape it so perfectly. I'd never swallow the paint on purpose, in fact, I'd always attempt to spit it out. I'd carefully scrape the flake from the nail and with my tongue wipe it on my hand or flick it out into the air. I wasn't an elegant child. All teeth, all grit, gimme that gold metallic cheapness in a crooked sheet, right off my nail, compliments of my top and bottom front teeth. Like a brown bear who's found a tent full of snacks behind the pine tree in December. It may all sound so violent and raw, but that's how it felt sometimes.

Why didn't I seek snacks? Because it wasn't about hunger—it was about the sensation on my teeth and the dysregulated signals between my brain and nervous system. The nail-biting became craftmanship over time. The teeth knew how to glide, crunch, rip, and peel a fingernail or a cuticle in a sort of unrehearsed choreography. And with my teeth action my nerves simmered down. So as grew older and the habit never stopped, I realized when I did grow my nails, I had to replace the habit with sugar, exercise, sewing, writing, chewing gum, or writing. Nail-biting habit held and still at times, holds so much power in my life, to the point where my chewed nails became part of my identity. Nail biters notice other nail biters and we understand the frenzy of it all. We understand the why, how and when. Are we anticipating an event? Did we just get awesome news? Are we changing plans? Do we sense danger? Rejection? Excitement? All reasons to chomp.

Such satisfaction when that one cuticle or thin flap of skin gets removed with the precision of a tiny manicure scissor. But now it's in your mouth. I can't even count the times I've bitten my nails down so far where it hurts to pick up items. Yet, that pain was a reminder of sensation and pressure-relief in some zig-zagged way. Like I had accomplished the ultimate level of nail-biting. It hurt, but I liked it.

One time a contemplative Chinese massage therapist told me I was missing certain vitamins in my body, but because my head was smooshed into the head-hole, I couldn't ask more questions. That freaked me out. I can go a year or more without biting. But God forbid a nail just seems too asymmetrical in a moment of anxiety about an upcoming life event. She will be bent and removed with my teeth, like an underperforming soldier or gymnast or whomever is part of a squad. And a few of its teammates are sure to follow, until eventually the entire team is wiped out. To be replaced by growing them from scratch once again.

My brother used to freak out. "Mom, she's got her feet in her mouth again!" It's true. Probably until I was about eight years old, I'd bend my leg and bite my toenails with prodigious energy. That kind of nail-biting involved the sense of stretch too. My legs—god how I love the pull of my muscles as they open and surrender to a stretch. So now we have that plus the nail bite. Please don't put the book down. This was a real part of my childhood, and sensory people are very creative people. I feel that it's all tied together to give us the ability to describe such human tendencies, from the odd to the average. From the bizarre little seconds to the strange moments in life.

The combination of the stretch of my leg and the fact that I enjoyed the smell of my toe skin made me a toenail biter for a brief period of my life. This was topped off with the bizarre mission to get every toenail the same length and off via teeth. Freakshow or totally human? I stopped biting my toenails around the age of eight because it's not hygienic, and I learned that quickly. I didn't get sick or anything. I simply realized it was ... gross. My feet were everywhere, then in my mouth? The wonder of it disappeared when I looked at myself in the mirror while chewing, and I saw the absurdity.

A few years later, I developed a little obsession with removing the hair on my legs efficiently and in the way the other girls did—their legs glistened and shone in the sun. My follicles were chestnut-brown dots—impossible to make go away during puberty. Until I learned about the disposable razor truth—they worked ten times better than the electric ones I used for fifth through seventh grade. Also, the shaving creams were crap back then. I wasn't a super hairy Italian. None of the women in my family have much, but the wispy patch on my shins and the sides of my calves made my head hurt. Meaning: It wasn't smoothed down or completed. It had to be vanquished. Imagine a Pac-Man board with one dot left, then you die. Yep.

The neighbor sisters who lived behind me on Mulberry had the shiniest, glossiest legs you'd ever lay eyes on. How? I wondered. It was tough enough for me, socially, that they had long, luscious legs with just the right amount of muscle, but now to have perfected the look of a waxed leg? It made a medium height, athletic-built girl feel inferior. Until of course, I could outrun all the girls in the neighborhood and many of the boys. I was lean for sure, but my legs weren't long, luscious, or shiny. I didn't know about lotion so much back then, and I am sure my mom tried to show me, but I was too impatient to learn. Or more likely, the lotion felt oily and was too much for my nose to take in all day.

The habit that began young and in front of John Ritter and Joyce DeWitt of *Three's Company* in the summer evenings was my body-twisting, particularly my hips and legs. I'd rarely sit or lay on my couch in front of the TV. I was a full-blown floor kid. I'd position my back against the couch or in the following positions: two legs bent in a sitting position so that my feet touched my bum, laying on my side facing the TV with my outer leg stretched up or out as far as it would go to feel the burn of the stretch, then switch sides, or finally on my stomach with my head back toward my toes from my bent knees under my body. I'd test my stretch constantly, but primarily because it just felt so damn good to do it—again, input, decompression, relief from something I couldn't verbalize. Sensory regulation equaled a body and mind that were in sync. If I was feeling adventurous, I'd put both legs over my head in the air, holding myself up at my hips, then bend them so my feet touched the ground behind me. On these occasions, I'd only be able to listen to the antics in the California apartment of Jack, Chrissy, and Janet. Or the sharp, witty remarks by Alan Alda's Hawkeye on my dad's favorite show, *M.A.S.H.* We didn't have air conditioning, so if it was summer, I was in my underwear watching TV, probably until about age ten. It was humid, carpeted, and an oven in the house, and it was the only way to be comfortable.

In spite of it all, and above all other twisting forms of input, my teeth are still what I turn to if I can't open or twist something like a bottle cap on a water bottle, or a package made of plastic. Only now, I remind myself that it's not a great idea, so the object rarely makes it to my mouth. I hear my mom's voice—"Here, give it to me. Don't use your teeth! You'll crack them." I have yet to crack a tooth, but I am also a grown-up whose teeth may not be the best choice of tool for opening plastic objects. I have access to jar openers and hands.

According to the National Association for the Education of Young Children (NAEYC), there are several reasons a child could bite, and so from their list, I pulled the reasons that I know were my reasons as a child. My list goes as follows: experience the sensation of biting, satisfy a need for oral-motor stimulation, feel strong and in control, and to express feelings of frustration and fear. Not fear of anyone, but more the situation of being cramped in a space like a car. As for my grandmother's chair, it's likely I didn't have enough art supplies nearby to express myself. According to a similar article put out by the *Chicago Parent* and via the University of Chicago, chewing on things often points directly to sensory issues. I had sensory issues.

That feels good to say.

I. Have. Sensory. Issues.

Walnut Street

I attended Walnut Street School in suburban Toms River, New Jersey from kindergarten through sixth grade, way before sixth grade was designated the first part of middle school years. It gave us the chance to be the top of the pyramid, foregoing the too-early exposure to making out, second base, and French kissing. Sure, it was around us, but not at the high-speed staccato of middle school. No tongue-poking happened on the playground of Walnut—only talk of it, or gossip that people were doing that in the woods by the cemetery after school. On the bus I heard that the F word meant two butts touching, and that kissing involved a lot of tongue, but my crowd wasn't so into that yet. We were still into neighborhood bike circles, whiffle ball tourneys, and ice skating at the town rink on Friday nights. Jaime Zazzara and I would ride our bikes every day in April and May to hang out with our prospective "love" interests. Their neighborhood was a few miles away from ours, and just past Walnut Street's back soccer fields. We never left our bikes. We'd talk and lean, whatever, but we'd never get closer to BJ and Mike than we were to each other on our ten speeds with our feet planted on the ground, our bikes leaning between our legs, acting like a safety net for awkwardness. The bike lean deserves a rock-solid spot in the charts of 1980s sociology—it was a pose, a state of being, and a comfort zone.

One of my very first memories of elementary school was a fresh Number 2 pencil point breaking then settling in to live in the palm of my hand for eternity. It was in the early morning before kindergarten and early in the school year because I remember that sun-filled chill in the air. I walked next door to the Martin's house because Dave Martin also attended Walnut Street kindergarten, and my mom had to go to work early that day. I remember his house smelled delightfully of scrambled eggs. I also remember it being the very first time I saw anyone put ketchup on scrambled eggs. I had already eaten my cereal at home, but I watched him eat his egg breakfast in pure fascination. Other people had weekday breakfast routines that involved eggs and bacon like on TV sitcoms. I began sorting through my supply box in my backpack before the bus came. I must've grabbed an extra sharpened pencil that was point up because the next thing I knew there was a bright red dot of blood where the pencil point had punctured my hand—the part of the palm between the thumb and index finger on my right hand, but closer to the index finger. It stung. I dabbed the blood with a wet paper towel and hadn't yet realized that the tip of graphite was now under my skin and would remain there forever. The initial sight of it scared me, but I had to get on the bus. I can still see the graphite dot the size of a Lyme tick super faintly now in my late forties. Perhaps it gave me the superpower to put words on paper.

At school, I made all kinds of friends in all kinds of socioeconomic situations, and I learned who and how I wanted to be as I grew older. In terms of my sensory stuff, I'm not sure where to begin. Maybe the beginning was the smell of the white gloopy paste that exited the bottle. The Elmer's Paste dried across my palms and caked to my eaten-up fingernails and papers where I dropped a good teaspoon too many on the construction paper basket or cake or bumblebee where it rose too high above the surface. Playing with excess paste was fun—always use more than the instructed amount. And it had a desserty smell, even taste. We've all sampled at least a few particles of the stuff at some point. Glue was elegant if applied properly, but this thick white frosting made for messy, uninformed art and task completion, and I loved every minute of it. Those bottles would get stuck shut after a few uses. What a waste of resources really.

"Ms. Braica, my paste won't open. It's stuck."

"Ask Jesse to share hers." Because of course the less scrappy peers kept tidy paste cylinders. It was only when the paste was passed out in class randomly that I had a fresh start—a chance to keep mine tidy too. It rarely happened though because you can't put a lid on a scrappy, chaotic artist, even in second grade. If it wasn't all over my fingertips, art didn't happen.

Mrs. Seip was my art teacher most years. She was a tiny-framed woman and had a very gender-neutral haircut which I loved her for—instinctually I knew it meant she was not afraid of her individuality. She often dressed in a cornflower blue cardigan, minimal makeup, and long pants. She taught us how to use all of the crayon colors and press down like your life depended on it. Broken ones. New ones. "Color thick and hard." Then we were instructed to cover all of it in black crayon with great magnitude. The pressure we used with the black crayons would matter. The pressure of the crayon to paper gave me joy and relief. Pushing down on anything brought relief. I never processed that this was happening, as I only see it in retrospect. I knew that it felt good to my developing nervous system. With short circuits all over the place, anytime I could achieve balance, was a win.

"Okay, very carefully, open your scissors. Use the less sharp blade and scratch over the black to reveal the colors underneath. Make designs to your heart's desire." The metal scissors with the green handles were for lefties. The plain metal ones, for righties.

The pressure necessary on the vivid crayon colors was another way to get my attention and keep it. A sort of strong load off the day's worries, pressed into beige, thick art paper. Crayon wax rammed into paper that smelled like school.

Music class was second best because of those red and green wooden sticks and the noise made by tapping two together to the beat of Mrs. Bentley's "Ta ta te te ta." Festive beats every Friday to the pace of her direction. Her spittle at the end of her mouth. She seemed eighty years old to us, but was probably only forty at the time. Mrs. Bentley fell into the legendary category of teachers, for she owned her craft and had us all convinced that her and that old wooden piano she wheeled around was all you needed to get by. It held secrets and sorcery, and music was the root of it—foundational, pure, and the building blocks of beat and time signature.

Gym class was a circus of senses once a week, as we always began with the primitive sound-system crackling the tune of "Chicken Fat" at the direction of Mr. Seip (the art teacher's fully-bearded husband) and Mrs. Konyhas. Why was it that everyone saved their gas for gym class? Suddenly everyone had to fart, and if it was taco day, it was also "I might lose my own lunch day" if the kid in my squad got too close to me during the jumping jack portion of "Chicken Fat." "Chicken Fat" was the quintessential warm-up routine that began with a march then progressed into jumping jacks, a jog-in-place, and push-ups. Our gym teachers would lead us, whistles around their necks, a twinkle in their eye. "Come on kids. Go you chicken fat, go away!"

It didn't take long for my senses to then introduce me to next-level feelings. First grade was when I first discovered my capacity for boy-craziness. And also when I realized that maybe he thought I was cute too. I never told anyone that I thought Danny Balance was cute, but he must've picked up on it. In the chaos of pack-up time and students buzzing in and around the accordion style coat closet that was perpetually stuck or wide open, Danny put his hand over my mouth and nudged me toward the closet. He then slapped a wet, sweaty, boy kiss on my cheek. His skin and breath smelled like red cherries. The whole situation was aggressive and strange, and never happened again. I hope he has learned consent by now. I'm not sure I ever told anyone about that. I remember the smells. The gut shivers.

In third grade Mrs. Moreau wrote our independent seatwork on the chalkboard and while she met with reading groups, the rest of us were left to complete these tasks to then be placed in a divided basket or tray, clearly labeled by subject. One of my favorite independent choices was to work in a Scholastic brand reading workbook while listening to a woman's voice through chunky headphones that weighed as much as me through an even clunkier cassette player. But that woman's voice. Like the middle-America grandmother I never had, nor truthfully ever needed since mine were queens, but I loved her voice. Like baked chocolate chip cookies and a glass of milk. She told me when to turn the page, when to fill in my answers, and when to review my answer choices. I loved the tidy process and her cookie texture vocals. Nothing felt more satisfying during those independent work phases than gliding a freshly sharpened pencil between the workbook lines provided for my answers. Answers to questions like, "Where was Mr. Barnes all morning?" Or "Why did Mrs. Sanchez walk so quickly?" He was at the bank working, and she was late for her dentist appointment. Questions in the comprehension check arena were thin in the 1980s. Currently, they're thick, challenging, and full of nuance. I wasn't exposed to anything about context or inference until high school.

Billy was one of the first boys in my childhood who alerted me to a more sophisticated brand of magnetism. He had a muscular body for an eleven-year-old boy, and freckles on his cheeks for miles. To make things more enticing, his hair flipped up at the end, almost at his shoulder. Not a mullet, as the sides were wavy, but not short. He was a very sexy kid for a fifth grader. He knew his charm, and he understood what girls liked. He knew how to flirt. My guess is that Billy had an older brother at home giving him all sorts of bad 1980s advice about girls. The difference between Billy in fifth grade and Adam in first, was that he had more manners. He wasn't very academic, and I was overly academic, so therefore, he was a "bad boy." He definitely liked me and I thought he was adorable, but scaredy-cat me never walked past him or said his name the way the other girls did. I simply connected to boys with my athletic ability, and I did just fine getting their gaze that way. I wanted to be known more for my speed than my lips. It worked, but then when I got their attention, I couldn't walk the walk or know what to do with it. So I moved on to other boys, and I paid more attention to my friends.

I remember so many girls from elementary school because I was and still am totally interested in how other people go about their days—meaning, did their moms make them splash their faces with cold water and Coast soap every morning? Were they allowed to eat Fruit Loops for breakfast like I wasn't? One particular girl who caught my attention and my empathy was named Melanie. I can even tell you where her bus stop was. That's how curious I was—or nosy. Take your pick. But your choice reflects more about you, not me. I genuinely cared about her. Back to Melanie. She was the girl who had more on her shoulders than any third grader should've. I could just tell. I could tell that she wasn't sure if she'd have a hot dinner, or if her mom would even be home when she needed her to be. She was a thick and tall girl. And why does that matter in this recollection? It matters because I could tell, even as a kid, that her weight literally weighed on her and made her partly who she was. Defensive, ready to pounce if anyone yelled "Melanie lives in a dumpy house behind McDonald's." My heart both filled and broke for her at the same time. I wanted to befriend her and let her know I thought she was fabulous, and in a weird way I was super jealous of her freedom and her maturity. That was my privilege stirring. It admittedly took me decades after that to truly understand. The child who is super cared for wanting the independence of the ones who aren't wholly noticed or taken care of in essential ways. I romanticized her struggles comparing her to Punky Brewster or Jo from *Facts of Life*, or maybe the poor neighbor friend of Samantha Micelli's. There was no conversation or honesty about privilege back then. Melanie wore blue eyeshadow in fourth grade. I found Melanie to be admirable in the way she tried to hide her insecurities over a facade of calm and confidence. Because to survive, she had to. Survive. There were many girls like Melanie on my bus. Pulled from the warmth of pure suburban coddle. On the perimeter of comfort. But did I befriend her, truly? Never enough to my best recollection. I know I tried to, but it was met with suspicion on her part and my other friends, and a kid of nine doesn't always know what to do with that suspicion. I wish I was braver back then. I wish I was brave enough to tell her how fabulous I found her.

Somewhere between kindergarten and third grade my class took a field trip to our local planetarium at the community college in town known as Ocean County Community College. The planetarium trip was popular and highly anticipated. It was a very quick bus ride down a major highway from Walnut Street School to OCC's parking lot. I was carsick, but it was brief because I was overjoyed and couldn't wait to see the night sky in the middle of my day with all of my excited school friends. The man's commanding voice boomed through the planetarium auditorium, explaining to us the stars we were seeing, the season we were experiencing, and the planets that swirled beyond our eyes. I loved feeling like it was autumn at night. It felt creepy and thrilling when the voice said, "The autumnal equinox will come year after year." I lived for that kind of echo. I loved the idea of being part of the Earth from that vantage point in my seat next to my friends. I was dizzy and a shade of green from the wide screen and lights dominating the indoor theater, but I ignored it. I refused to let it bug me in that moment because I was more amped up than anything else. That's the thing about childhood sometimes. Adrenaline becomes our friend often, and it allows us to be free for just a second with our friends.

I remember the satisfaction of soft chalk on a clean chalkboard in Mrs. Lees' fourth grade class. Close your eyes. Imagine a brand-new piece of ten-inch yellow chalk. Caress it. Now press it onto a spotless green chalkboard. Make a tall line. It's heaven, right? Right?

In fourth grade, Mrs. Lees gave us independent time daily, and once we finished our work and she met with various reading groups we could pick our enrichment task from the selection she chose. One of the activities a group of us became obsessed with was a box of flashcards likely published in the 1950s. Based on its font, colors, and simplicity, these were old cards. Every card had a state outlined in muted red ink so you could discern its shape and bordering states. Listed below the states' outlines were the following: the capital, largest city, and nickname with matching graphics in the same red ink. Over the course of what felt like months looking back, but was probably only a few weeks, me and a group of about four friends, memorized all fifty states and their facts. I can't explain how, but these flashcard sessions were an antidote to my sensory stuff too. Maybe it was the categories and the checklist quality that more suited me as a kid who needed boundaries and expectations? But also, the nicknames were something that helped me visualize the states: the Sunshine State, the Garden State, the Show-Me State, the Empire of the South. I could see the emoji for each before I knew what an emoji was, you know? It could've been the repetitive nature of the information, day after day. I knew what to expect. I knew Pennsylvania would be the Keystone State every day, despite not knowing what keystone meant.

Later that same year, our entire class sculpted a six-foot clay model of New Jersey. Mountains, plateaus, hills, and swamp, all molded and bent from difficult-to-manipulate modeling clay offered in bulk packaging probably shipped from a warehouse in Iowa. It was greenish-gray in its original form, and to even remove it from the other chunks in the packaging was a challenge. Our fingernails must've been clogged for days, but god damn, our souls elevated. At least, mine was. The pinching and gripping was hearty, and the end results—dried water-based Tempura paint slopped and brushed over dried clay like inedible cake. Gorgeous, thick, and sliceable.

Sixth grade took place in Mr. Huber's classroom on the second floor of Walnut Street School. Mr. Huber was a pleasant man, softspoken, and interested in our success. It was the teacher across the hall though, that fulfilled my sensory stuff. Mrs. Scaglione. They had assessed our math abilities using a very basic math test, and I tested a smidgeon above average, but not enough. This meant I remained with my own teacher, Mr. Huber. Well, after two weeks of whizzing through all the math work, and being done way before everyone else, he moved me up to Ms. Scaglione's class across the hall. Now, I was with all my friends who were in the Gifted and Talented program. The one I never could test into. Ms. Scaglione had a certain affect. Her voice sounded buttery; the slow, graceful way she moved mesmerized. She made math seem so ... simple and velvety. And of course, her chalk always stroked the board so softly and smoothly, never a tap or scratch. Always a glide and a shiver up the board. I lived for it. And the way she formed her numbers was flawless. It made me learn. Ms. Scaglione, similar to the Scholastic lady on the cassettes, had a very comforting delivery, albeit, more serious than Grandma Scholastic. She was also younger and a new teacher, clearly determined to teach us advanced math well. She spoke. We listened. I remember she had high, plastered bangs like many of us girls, and long fingers that maneuvered that soft chalk so very beautifully to my eyes and ears.

○

Sixth grade was the same year Jaime and I rode our bikes to see BJ and Mike after school for an hour or two before they had baseball practice and we had dancing school. They both lived on Evelyn Court in our town. The outfit I recall so vividly that year was my pair of aqua blue shimmer spandex pants under a pair of black-and-white boxer shorts. The shorts were baggy and street-arty, almost like graffiti. It was all very quintessential 1988 United Outlet chic. I wish I had a photo to recall this perfectly. The two parts of my sixth grade look that never changed were my hair and my wrists. Banana clips were the choice for my thick, frizzy hair, and my wrist sported a thick-banded POP Swatch, neon pink cloth with writing in white and yellow. It said SWATCH. Above that huge watch was another thin plastic Swatch watch. Yes, I wore two watches. The sensory memory I have about this look was the smell. We rode our bikes so hard in the sun, and I ran my life away, in general—in the neighborhood, around the school grass, everywhere—that my perspiration was daily and constant. Mix that with the Exclamation perfume I wore, and you have a cloth watch wristband that smelled a certain way. Fruity, sweaty tween? You bet. And in moments, that smell would calm me down. If I was nervous or unsure, I'd sniff it the same way a toddler might sniff their security blankie.

Walnut Street School, I love you forever.

The Garage

So much of my early sensory self happened in our hot, single-car garage on Mulberry Place. It was a tidy garage, maybe a tad bigger than our small kitchen. It served as another room for my brother and I to occupy and be kids in—a space to bounce our basketballs, pump bike tires, and juggle endless tennis balls unsuccessfully. The one-car garage also served as my dad's entertainment room of sorts. Through the years it housed his stained-glass equipment, neon beer signs, go carts, dartboards, motorcycles, and sports equipment. All bundled and stacked in wooden boxes, metal shelves, and plastic containers. Everything arranged precisely enough to make Marie Kondo blush and hold my dad's iced tea.

My dad was a drill sergeant in the US Army Reserves from 1968 until 1971. His army hat and jacket hung on a hook in the garage near the laundry room doorway. Eventually, I'd high-jack that jacket and wear it all over college campus in the fall of 1996 until about 1998.

My dad knew how to organize a space to the best of its potential. Other than the garage, we had only a small attic for storage. It was in the hallway upstairs between my brother's room and mine, and we knew when that door opened that it was one of two occasions—our dad reorganizing the boxes, or it was early December and we were about to decorate our tree. The attic resembled the garage. Squarely tidy, labels on everything, and every item stored tightly. This was my dad's tidying of his sensory processing issues. To create space for items and belongings in a way that de-cluttered his living area was his mode of regulation—one that I adopted and continue to both fight and celebrate, depending on the day of the week.

We didn't have a basement on Mulberry Place, but we had the attic and a high functioning, super organized, multi-faceted garage designed and upkept by a former drill sergeant. The door leading from the laundry room in the house out to the garage was a typical heavy wooden door with a brass knob. It was an impossible fit and poorly designed, meaning—if both the laundry room door that opened to the inside of our house and that heavy brown garage door were both opened up at the same time: collision, curse words, and crushed fingers resulted. All did, many times. It's probably the largest source of my parents' "Shits!" and "god damn its!"

My mom never loved the layout of the house, but it was my childhood home, and I'll love it until the day I die. I think she appreciated how well the house treated us, but little things like too-close doors made things difficult for adults. The clicking and clacking and beating against one another made for poor transitions from once space to another, especially when one person didn't realize the other was coming through. Or when you had an armful of groceries or laundry.

My dad's stained-glass hobby is an early garage memory. The metal pieces that bent for the outline of the shape. My dad's specialties were grape bunches, pears, apples, triangular Christmas trees, and classic candlesticks with a ring for holding it. He'd cut the glass, melt the metal outline strip, and bend it to hold in the colored glass. I wish I asked to try it, but he was super meticulous, so any wasted mistakes would've been too risky. He'd add hooks and suction cups to the final projects. Those of you who grew up in the '80s will recall they were a popular decoration on windows of all sizes and shapes. He bought his supplies from a shop in a small beach town called Bayhead on Bridge Ave. There he'd pick the guy's brain about set-up and materials, and he'd figure out the rest on his own. He'd score and cut the glass into shapes that made for delightful window ornaments. The slice of metal band, cracks and lines so exact, fitting together *or* apart like a symphony.

On the left wall, looking in from the outside of the garage, on a tightly affixed hook, was a dartboard set comprised of three yellow darts and three red darts. The grip part of the dart was bumpy and silver. The feel, the trajectory, and the physics. These were sharp, adult darts, not magnets. And they were placed in a holder inside the two-door wooden vest-like cabinet. It was positioned between the bikes hanging on rubber ceiling hooks the size of hands and our garage phone. The dartboard fulfilled two main purposes: to give my brothers' friends and I a chance to hold dart tournaments, and a space for solo dart meditation to the sound of the local radio station. Those red darts reminded me of solid Kool-Aid, so of course, they'd find their way to my teeth on occasion. The yellow resembled the yellow in our bird's crest.

My dad had painted the most perfect shiny navy-blue square in the middle of the garage floor, closer to his workbench on the end of the garage away from the driveway. Was it to imitate the pit area where mechanics work? It was. In case oil or coolant or whatever else dripped out of cars, the painted surface was glossy and easier to scrub than the unfinished cement that simply soaked up the car oils and chaos. The navy-blue paint sealed the rock. Suburban efficiency was John Battista's specialty.

My dad's one workbench area included a back pegboard wall where he'd easily hang his drills and lamps and anything else. His toolbox and other sets of tiny plastic drawers held nails, screws, washer, nuts of all sizes. I remember a surplus of caps the same tiny sizes of every color, and I do not remember seeing those caps anywhere in life but in those drawers. They almost looked like his beloved chiclets from the gumball machines in our house. Greens, yellows, reds, and blues. Like they could fit on every toe. Fast forward to six months ago when I decided to ask my dad what they were—wire caps. They group and fasten wires in an organized way. Organization *within* organization.

Every tiny plastic drawer had a label made from the label maker that was out of my reach. He knew. He knew I'd use it, probably chew it, and get its money's worth. I know my dad found his own sensory and textural satisfaction in not only creating the labels, peeling them from their sticker, but also from seeing them so perfectly displayed on each drawer telling the audience what sat where, likely never to be needed. Maybe his own father and uncles and cousins in Newark and Staten Island had arranged their garages the same way. Maybe it was all a nod to his roots. I am one hundred percent certain that this kind of radical organization was to ease his own sensory distress. The neatness kept his nerves in check.

The wooden sports bin that sat against the wall of the garage was a basic square box about three feet tall, made of unfinished wood with a hinge lid. It didn't slam shut—my dad likely rigged it to have the tension it needed to preserve our fingers when reaching in to grab our basketballs, baseballs, and the other crap we stuffed in it—Madballs, tennis rackets, jump ropes, and soccer balls. The unfinished wood helped the smell of the garage, of course. Cedar-delicious. I could've bathed in those smells all day long. There was something so familiar and soothing for me about the wood scents. Perhaps in my past life I was a termite. Or even more glamourous, a woodpecker.

One main sensation I remember about our garage was sweat on my skin. Productive, happy sweat that beaded, puddled, or dripped, depending on the catalyst. The garage was the origin of a sped-up pulse and heartbeat for the following reasons:

Music video, door closed: I'd bring my boom box into the garage from the house—rest it up as high as I could reach while climbing the faux wooden shelves held up by real metal. Usually I'd get it just a few feet above my head, thinking the position would offer a better boom into the space. If my mom's Oldsmobile was in the driveway, this space was mine for the taking. "So Emotional" by Whitney Houston was a popular video, as was "Control" by Janet Jackson. My choreography had a lightning tight pop about it, softened around the edges by a creamier ballet leg extension segue. I paid attention to the experts on how to balance a performance. Too much of any one style got tedious and boring to watch. I'd surprise my pretend audience of shovels and rakes with sheer emotion. I'd be dripping in sweat because there was no ventilation in the middle of winter.

Exercise in summer, door open: This was my chance to show random around-the-neighborhood walkers how prepared I was for show business. These routines with the door open had a more repetitive flavor, like the warmups I'd learned at my dancing school. If I was in motion, it was a performance. If I felt my calves and thighs burn, I was doing it all right. I knew tonight was pizza English muffin night, and I would devour at least four of them, so I channeled my inner Jennifer Beales and maniack-ed my way around the open garage to something like "Let's Hear it for the Boy" or "Rhythm of the Night" by DeBarge until the burning hit my legs and the thick August air filled my lungs. I craved that point of difficult, and only realized *why* much later in my adult life. The input. The anxiety-wipe.

Weights: My dad had a set of free weights—a goldish-brown color, and probably they were too heavy for me to be lifting especially when technique and safety wasn't in the 1980s kid vocabulary.

Sunset, cool breeze, hint of humid: The perfect opportunity to pick up the phone in the garage and call my friends. Yes, my dad installed a phone in the garage. It was highly beneficial when I started calling boys I liked around the age of thirteen. While I chatted, to soothe my nerves, I'd press my nose against the overused basketball that needed constant air refills or my baseball glove. God I loved the smell of that thing—leathery, summery dirt.

The sound of crickets at night while in the garage was one of my favorite sounds. It meant the day was winding to a close, but also that the sun wasn't so far away. Though I am a true winter lover now, summers were for kids in the 1980s, and all decades, for that matter. Our summer evenings on Mulberry Place were infused with punchy barbecue smells from Joe Skiba's charcoal grill that he used in the driveway. He'd stand out in his old white T-shirts, socks and sandals and poke the meat around. He seemed so old to me, but he was probably only about forty. The summers in my neighborhood choked on those charcoal smells, the smell of basketballs on our hands in our friends' driveways, and the smell of our sweat from the long days outside in empty wooded lots and hot crunchy-rocked streets. All from the vantage point of my 1980s garage floor.

Mork, My Man

Mork from Ork was my husband. You pulled his little cord with the white plastic ring on the end and he'd utter "Nanu, Nanu." I designated him my husband when I was six. He was eighteen-inches in body length and sported a painted set of overalls and striped shirt—true to his *Mork & Mindy* appearance on TV he had his signature suspenders, Robin Williams face, and denim pants. All mine. My best guess is that my parents saw him in Toys R Us and knowing how much I enjoyed the sitcom, bought it for me. The other guess is that I used my own birthday money from relatives and picked him off the shelf myself.

Technically speaking, a Robin Williams doll joined me everywhere I went. Sitting on the orange upholstered chair at a colleague of my dad's house drinking a grape soda and talking about school with the adults was one situation I found myself in during the Mork-doll years. His goofy presence comforted me. I'd cross his floppy legs in the most realistic way possible. The feel of his cloth body against my hands. The sound of his Nanu, Nanu. Both the touch and sound of the doll made me feel at ease in new situations. I think his stuffed head was designed much too big for his body—his floppy legs attached at this rectangular torso of a body. But again, he was all mine, and we were married.

"Oh how cute your little girl is. Is that her doll?"

"He's my husband. Mork. See." Cord pulled. Nanu, Nanu. I was proud, and the feel of his fabric gave me more comfort than I can explain.

I must remember to thank my parents for not judging me too hard and for letting me take him out of the car and into the homes of the people we were visiting. If you're not familiar with *Mork & Mindy*, here's the quick summary paraphrased from the *Mork & Mindy* fandom website.

Mork is a member of a race of humanoid life-forms, known as Orkans, from the planet Ork, sent to Earth to observe and report back on human behavior who is befriended by Mindy McConnell, an Earth Girl who helps shelter, guide, and teach him about the ways of Earthlings, and especially their emotions. Living with her in her apartment he forms a strong friendship with her, falling in love with her, proposing to and marrying her.

Mork's character is highly endearing, and you want to be his friend from the moment you meet him. He's kind, friendly, and very willing to learn the ways of human behavior. I adored the way Robin Williams developed the character, in turn, making us fall in love. Did I see a trait in Mork that I wanted in a friend, or was I simply mesmerized by the fantasy of a humanoid life-form being as emotional as real humans? Mork, a la Robin Williams, had hairy arms, a cake-sweet smile, and crystal blue eyes.

My Mork from Ork attachment makes me wonder why kids cling to objects, or why they're drawn to characters from TV. Why do we require that thing in our hands, our grip, near our noses to feel organized and at ease from setting to setting. Blankies, dolls, pieces of fabric, whatever it may be that gives humans the feeling of comfort and home. Why do we run to their refuge in our beds or on our sofas and hold them tighter than life?

My youngest daughter carries her blanket around the house from the time she wakes up until she gets dressed, and then sleeps with it again at night. She does it more frequently when she's feeling uncertain or uneasy about an upcoming event. During the first six months of COVID in 2020 when the whole world was quarantined, she had her blankie by her side always. There's a ridge of the blanket that she prefers and rubs her thumbs over for comfort. She's shown me the technique and then has asked me to try it. There's comfort for her in the sensory experience of this soft fleece yard of fabric. The smell and the touch give her a feeling of security and familiarity. I had a plain white cotton piece of cloth when I was five years old, and I'd bring it on trips to Bradlees and Best, and I suppose it's comparable to my little one's blankie.

Bradlees was an old department store, always standalone, not in malls, and it smelled like perfume and salty cardboard. The heat was always jacked up too high, and my mom spent way too long looking for shoes and bargains on blouses. My cotton piece of cloth kept me from losing my bearings, I'm sure of it. Over-stimulus and the combo of the heat and smells marched behind me in Bradlees, but my cloth acted like a shield.

Mork was different from a blankie, though. Yes, his texture comforted me, but I think it was also about the world I'd created in my mind. The reality that wasn't. Fantasy authors will relate to this. He was my companion that wasn't human. An opportunity to oversee a creative place in the corner of my heart and spirit. I built a world! A made-up scenario that imitated what I saw happening in the lives of my older babysitters and uncles. Going out to eat, bowling nights, having people over for cake and coffee, and maybe a getaway to somewhere like Atlantic City to play slot machines. Atlantic City overnight was the glamourous date night tryst of the '80s. My point of view was simply a six-year-old with nothing but a Mork from Ork doll as a husband and parents with a robust social and family life. He traveled up and down the Garden State Parkway with me and my family, and nobody flinched.

Why was it so important to me to have a partner? I think I saw how it worked well for my parents. Their decisions about where to go for their day off were interesting to me, and I noticed that if my mom had the last word, everyone was pleased. If the decisions made it through the matriarchal checklist and quality control meter, our day would be delightful. But my dad was made for it, and it worked well for his disposition. I remember the two personalized zodiac plaques they had displayed in our garage. Scorpio and Libra, my dad being the latter. I remember connecting the symbolism of the scales and the neatness that was my father. I also remember being a little bit afraid of the depiction of the Scorpio, yet how fierce it felt to have a mom who embodied its strength. Don't cross that venomous scorpion, ever. The two plaques, side by side, like my parents. Perhaps their zodiac signs sealed their fate, still being together since the early 1970s. What's funny about the plaques is that my aunt and uncle had mugs of the same sentiment. One for her—a Virgo earth mother with long hair and a look of "I will help you with everything and anything you will ever need in life," my uncle's a Libra too, so he too had a set of balanced scales. My aunt and uncle are together after fifty-plus years of marriage, and whether or not their signs even matter, it's a very early memory I have related to the inner workings of couple-dom.

As far as my texturally and creatively pleasing doll, Mork, I had decided he was the sign that best matches with my Aquarian heart. I didn't know anything about what my sign stood for, but I knew mine carried a huge vat or container of water to provide for others. In my heart, I assigned Mork as the perfect mug to match mine. The plaque. We'd have imaginary dinners at restaurants after long days at the beach with our friends. We'd invite friends for cake and coffee on Saturdays and chat about grown-up things.

I remember snagging my mom's zodiac paperback from her nightstand drawer—*Linda Goodman's Relationship Signs,* publication date 1970ish. I read it over and over, as it spoke about compatibility and the nature of the signs. That set up a lot of notions for me as a teenager, and you can be sure I became finely tuned to my friends' signs. It also might be responsible for why I can remember anyone's birthday if they tell me once. Fun fact: I'm most drawn to Aries, Sagittarius, Cancers, and Libras without evening thinking too hard about it. Tauruses seem to lurk in my hallways too, but they perplex and make me want to pull my eyeballs out of my head sometimes. Sorry, bulls. It's not always about you.

In the vein of dates and romance, there was one winner of a show that romanticized every notion of dating and love matches: *The Love Boat.* At every turn, the characters had dates on the giant cruise ship—out at dinner, pairing up and glammed up for a night of dancing or pure posing while eating. Women wore silky and slinky dresses and wet lipstick. Fingernails were painted in shimmery pinks, peaches, and reds. I was obsessed. The idea of a match between a set of people. Learning smells and touch language date after dinner date. Movie night after movie night. *Three's Company* portrayed a less glitzy, middle-class night life, or if I want to be more accurate—San Diego middle-class twenty-somethings who frequented the Regal

Beagle bar and restaurant. Always sunny, espadrilles in full effect. Janet and Terry always had the ultimate purse to pair with their shoes and double barrette combo, or in Janet's case—her black eyelined, purple shadowed eyes. As a kid I had the most detailed imagination when it came to pretending in my mind, that I was getting ready for a dinner date after a long day of either work at my aunt Connie's gift shop or a day tanning on the beach. (See the Nectarine Pit chapter too.) The funny thing was, I was more concerned about the anticipation, the blush, the lipstick, and the hair more than the date himself. Of course, until Mork came into my life. When I got too old to carry Mork around, you can bet your bottom dollar I had real crushes on boys. When I fell, I fell hard because of course the relationship world I built for me and Billy McMahon in my mind was more dramatic than anything in real life.

I remember Billy loved pancakes, so in my imagination, I would come to visit him on a Saturday morning before a game, and his mom would make us pancakes. We'd smile, laugh, and they'd comment how sweet of a girl I was, and how lucky Billy was to have met me. We were only eleven.

We cannot dismiss the idea of a kiss at the end of the date on my porch too. I have a distinct memory of showing my mom, what I labeled at age seven, the soap opera kiss versus the sweet kiss. The soap opera kiss went like this: plant the kiss on your person, then twist your mouth, still closed, from side to side. That is how I innocently processed what I saw on TV. So my mom would oblige and let me do it on her, as she laughed heartily. Then the sweet kiss: a peck on the lips, then a hug. Funny enough, I didn't practice on my Mork doll like the reader suspects. Only my mom got that love from me. Mork simply followed my lead from location to location. Did they let me bring him out to dinners in public at restaurants? It's possible, but I cannot remember. All I know is, Mork was my husband for a few months, then he got stuffed in my closet.

Nanu. Nanu.

Shops and Stickers

I think scratch and sniff stickers by Matte were essentially the first emojis. The colorful, touchable likeness of something that smelled and represented what you wished to express. Oh! Elaina loves that strawberry." "You have the jelly on bread? Rachel really wants that one." "The roller skate is the only one Teresa wants!" That kind of thing.

My favorite sticker from the classic Trend Matte scratch and sniff collection, by far, was the plump strawberry with the words Berry Good across its cheeky middle section. My second favorite was the pizza slice, titled Hot Stuff, and in third place, the set of two bananas exclaiming Appealing. The Melon Power watermelon slice and the chocolate ice cream cone, Super Scooper were next in line. It mattered because if I owned only one of them, it wasn't enough. We'd trade and wait. Trade and wait. These stickers repped the 1980s with both fragrance and style—nothing was subtle about them, and nothing was graceful. All slap, punch, and "here I am!"

There was a fruit-essence about being a kid in the 1980s. Everything smelled like fruit. Or looked like it smelled like fruit—jelly bracelets, jelly shoes, neon hair bows, chunky earrings and anklets, and most of our lip glosses hidden in the plastic representations of an orange slice or a strawberry.

Those lip glosses had ropes so they could double as necklaces. Even our fat shoelaces held specks of citrus limes and yellows. Kid-dom in the '80s burst with a color joy that can only be compared to having a fresh, thick sheet of white construction paper, a brand-new box of crayons, and sharp pencils at your desk. No homework. Just a clean canvas, and there you're off to create the prettiest rainbow you've ever seen on paper. The wax smell smeared across palms like a sacrament.

In the Ocean County Mall was a retail store called Pandemonium, nestled between Jo-Ann's Nuthouse and probably a clothing store like Copper Rivet. God, what I would pay to see a photo of the interior of Pandemonium right now, circa1986. Those glorious thick roles of stickers dominating the ceiling and tickling our faces as we browsed. It was a sight to see—a variety store streaming with literally dozens of rolls of stickers hanging around the register area in the center of the store, serving as the main attraction, and as decor. Rolls of stickers in the categories of hearts, oily unicorn heads, bananas, glitter stars, Hello Kitty faces, candy, music notes, pretzels, teddy bears, and on and on until your heart could explode confetti in the best of ways. On the floor were displays of journals, pens, erasers, Hello Kitty everything, wallets, and more stickers. Sticker books, stuffed unicorns, headbands, rainbow notebooks, and neon coin purses were displayed at every turn. Wow, the unicorn really was the mascot of the decade, wasn't it? This store was simultaneously a heaven and a hell for the olfactory and visually sensitive person. It made me happy more than not, that's what I remember. Any spare change I had from birthdays or Christmas, I spent here or at the record store. I remember spending at least thirty minutes just ogling before I chose my sticker or two from the rolls, and then deciding that my strawberry-gloss scented headache was the bane of my eight-year-old existence, and it was time to eat a Hot Sam pretzel to settle my stomach.

I grew up in New Jersey where large buildings were leased or purchased on major highways for hundreds of vendors to rent space the size of a bathroom and sell their items. Man their booths. Two come to mind—the Rt 18 Indoor Flea Market in Old Bridge and the Rt 9 Indoor Flea Market in Howell. In my kid memory there were hundreds of vendors, but my guess is that dozens is the more accurate unit of measurement. We'd often go on a Sunday morning, and we'd bundle up since it was cold concrete indoors with only space heaters in the booth areas. My dad always seemed to be on a mission to find toys from his childhood or Hess trucks when they were a hot collectible item. I was on the hunt for the latest Jordache purse. I'm pretty sure I owned a royal blue one, but what I really wanted was a hot pink one. Only, I don't think it ever happened that way. They'd have white or green, but not hot pink in stock, and it wasn't for not arriving early enough. My dad is known to open places. First ones there, or at latest, second. If you're on time, you're late.

The other place I remember being enamored by as a kid in a very prompt Italian-American family was Freedman's bakery near my house on Rt 166. We'd go for a loaf of rye bread, and maybe my brother and I would be allowed to choose a doughnut on a Saturday or Sunday morning. Freedman's shared an entrance with the Dover Pharmacy. Both places were delights for me—shelves of candies and breads and a back wall of school supplies. Arrays. I love neatly merchandized arrays. I enjoyed the likes of shoe stores, candy in drug stores, Smurf villages, and as mentioned earlier, the glory of Pandemonium.

Much later in my childhood, now venturing into puberty-plus territory, I was completely head over heels for Vogue magazines. In many ways, my fashion magazine habit replaced the sticker collecting. It was the new visual-artifact component of my life. Feeling renewed creatively over photos of garments that I'd never wear, but identities I could plug into my psyche for the rest of my womanhood. The way the models bent and posed gave me this feeling that it was okay to express myself in different ways, from my button-down shirts to my chunky boots with sundresses. I remember imitating a model with her shoulder-length hair, slicked back, more on the masculine bend. Her dress was long and fuchsia, split down the middle, with only two cutlets of fabric covering her breasts. I couldn't duplicate the outfit, but there was an attitude and a bravery about her stance: "I'm long, covered in coconut oil, and I live on the islands of Moon River. I only eat dragon fruit, and I can outrun you." She looked like she ruled the universe and no one could get in her way, yet she still seemed kind. I wanted to be her. Then other Vogue pages felt softer and like something more powdery and old: "I live in a ballet pink cottage off the coast of Maine, and I make saltwater taffy in heels." I wanted to be her too. If only those pages weren't drenched in strong perfumes. Even so, I bought them when I could, and flipped through them with eagerness all through high school. Sometimes, I'd rip pages out if I felt the photography spoke to me loud and clear, and I'd tape it on my bedroom wall, despite my Dad's insistence that the paint would peel and I'd destroy everything they worked hard for over the years. I required color. I required atmosphere. I required colorful chaos to quell the inner sensory chaos, so that in turn, the meld left my brain chemicals with balance and calm.

Brain in the Way

Karly Sandrino was a cheerleader for the Toms River Little Indians Pop Warner team when we were all in fourth grade together. We lived in a region near the beach, and a town who considered sports their church. You belong, you devote, and you win. Karly was part of the awesome group of friends that poured in from the neighboring town of Beachwood, a couple miles south of my town. They were awesome because they were more street smart and rebellious than my neighborhood—a certain quality of kid that didn't care about how many scratch-and-sniff strawberries filled their sticker books, but rather, did their little brother and sister eat dinner before their parents got home from work later at night?

Karly and a few other girls in my fourth-grade class cheered as Pop Warner cheerleaders for the football team known as the Toms River Indians. Tryouts were open to everyone, but I never bothered to ask my parents. They would never put that kind of commitment into our weekly pace—to dive into cheerleading that deeply—since I was already in dancing school. That was only once a week, but it was my passion, and it was what we could afford. In our shore region of state, sports were and still are queen, king, and everything in between. Ever since our Little League Championship in 1998 things have only amplified.

I was a dancer not a cheerleader, but oh my god, I wanted to be like Karly. So, I asked. I asked her to teach me the cheers, the routines, the movements. She did. In the hallways, in the cafeteria, anywhere in between when we had to stay silent or focus. She was so patient as my coach. B-E A-G-G-R-E-S-S-I-V-E I could tell she enjoyed my obsession with her Pop Warner cheerleader status and knowledge, and not in a snobby way. Her legs pointing and swirling were precise, strong, muscular, even more than mine, and I admit I was blessed with killer legs as a kid—not long and lean, but really defined. The kind of legs that took a girl far on the track against the boys. The legs that stood out in dance class for their conviction. I guess in a way I felt like a kindred spirit with girls who also had strong legs.

Cut to the newest fascination I adopted after learning all the cheers I could learn: the fluorescent, glittery back handspring. In my small Walnut Street Elementary school world, it was the mother of all ferocious endeavors as a girl in fourth grade. The choreography of the neck to hand to ground via legs, through sunshine, into clouds—in an order I could never grasp. Karly spotted my lower back with her hands, modeled the form of the leap, and verbalized the sequence of the handspring better than any fourth-grade girl ever could've. I couldn't bring myself to make the literal leap backwards. I couldn't bring myself to launch in the air. My back walkover was perfection because of the emphasis on the word *walk*. The sequence was crystal clear and made sense to me. I told myself it's the same move, just faster. It really wasn't. One is like ballet; the other is aerodynamics. If you think a lot, this move isn't for you.

The ingredient missing was risk. The ingredient I did not have in my heart, head, and the thing I could never locate was freedom. Jump back into the softness of earth. Let the hands and head lead. Yeah, well, my brain got in the way, and kept trying to tell me this wasn't natural and that I'd break my neck. My mom's voice, maybe? The thing about me mixed with risk was guilt. Fear of disappointing my mom dribbled through the crevices of my brain matter. The broken bones might result in a huge medical bill if I wasn't careful. I'd pulled my hamstring muscle pretty badly twice before turning eighteen, but muscles heal at no cost to a doctor or hospital visit. Bones require more visits, more hardware, and more follow-ups. What if the back handspring broke my wrist? What if my parents couldn't afford to get it fixed?

There were already enough risky things separating me and the Beachwood girls—early periods, French kisses, and shaved legs. Now I had to add back handspring to the list.

God knows this was all me though. They tried so hard on my behalf. Karly never broke her neck or back. Nicole DeFria never broke hers, and I know their parents wouldn't be able to afford that hospital bill either. I couldn't do it. I had the strength, the flex, the form, the coordination, but the follow through of the jumping into air behind me? Clearly that was reserved for the goddesses with cheer skirts. Girls with nothing to fear. Girls born to fly and defy gravity. It seemed to me that the bolder and braver girls

On the south side of town where these girls were from kids were more street smart. I didn't understand why then, but as an educated adult, I can understand the socioeconomics involved. The commonsense factor that happens more naturally when you have to fend for yourself more, and you have a little less to work with at home, or sometimes, a lot less resources.

I recently saw Karly in the main office of my daughter's school building as a substitute secretary. I could tell she had a sensibility about herself still, as adults. Same as when we were kids. Steps ahead.

"Hi Karly! Do you know I still think about that back handspring I could never do? No matter how patient you were with spotting me?"

She laughed. She remembered. But I know she will never write for twenty minutes about it because it was like breathing to her. Not something she tried to do every day for all of fourth grade and some of fifth. Some people fly. Others think too much about the sequence of a gymnastics move instead of trusting physics. Overthinkers aren't free. We live on a planet called "Whatcouldhappen."

I believe that those whose minds have trouble shutting off and taking a break to inhale the moment are the ones who often require the constant motion. The motion then forces the brain to take a backseat to the physical so you drive in freedom for a little while. So that you can eventually fall asleep at night. Again.

Newark

The kitchen took up a majority of Grandma Yola's house in Newark, as it was clearly designed at a time when multiple families lived in one house. The kitchen was the main conference room where all important events and celebrations took place—Sunday dinners, holidays, and basic cake and coffee evening get-togethers with nearby friends. I remember some of those too. Very faintly since she moved out when I was about ten years old. In that kitchen I learned the fine art of washing your hair in the kitchen sink. The way it cleans and refreshes a girl any time of day. You have nothing to wash but your hair, so it's like an exercise in precision and focus. I recall the bottle of my grandmother's Selsun Blue on the sink ledge. It made me feel safe and comfortable to see my grandmother's items spread about—she was active and in touch with her needs.

The other memories connected to this house in Newark was the trouble I caused, unscrewing after confiscating a bottle of black pepper from my grandmother's roll out drawer in the kitchen. I sprinkled it across her master bedroom floral comforter. It caused my aunt Rose, my mom, and Grandma Yola to race around the house to pinpoint why my cousin Peter, only a year younger than me at about five, was sneezing uncontrollably. I'm pretty sure I sat in wide-eyed silence in the kitchen, eating Stella Doro cookies, while they scrambled and yelled the way we do as Italians when the balance is disturbed. Even more mischievous was the time I locked myself in my grandmother's very pink and black tiled bathroom in that house. I know it wasn't to start trouble. It was to feel freedom and escape from the center of things. I knew at a young age that I was a bird with wings. You could not cage me then. You cannot cage me now.

"Elaina. Unlock the door, Elaina," my mom's voice shaking from the outside of the bathroom. "Can I come in now? It's mommy."

I was five years old or she would not have been so concerned about the kind of danger I could get into in a very porcelain and tile bathroom with a window above the clawfoot tub.

"Can you unlock the door for mommy?"

Two hours later, just before she picked up my grandmother's landline to call the police or fire department to crawl through the bathroom window to get me out, I gave in. I suppose I felt my independent time had been sufficient. I also know I was likely feeling overstimulated from the smells and energy of the house—grandma's veal on the stove, my mother's loud advice, my aunt's louder voice, and probably three other bursts of something I can't recall like music or the phone ringing, or Newark being Newark outside. Her gas stove burners were rich, left a stink, and I'm sure I retreated to the bathroom for reprieve.

o

It's Uncle Newark, Aunt Newark, Cousin Newark, Mother Newark. Both of my parents have deep roots from this city in northern New Jersey, and it's a permanent fixture in our lives, even when we all die. It begs for space in these pages. I've never lived in Newark, but apparently, my ancestors really hail from there above anywhere else in terms of heart and nerve endings. There's a serious pride that seeps out of the pores of Newark born-and-bred individuals, from my experience. It was a bustling epicenter during the 1940s and 1950s. Families lived very close to one another, and often in the same multi-family house. Butchers flourished. Chocolate factories thrived and spit out treasures by the pound. Retail stores kept consumerism booming. It was basically a New York City in north-eastern New Jersey, and only a thirty-minute drive into New York. It's also the home of a very large international airport.

My dad, aunt Connie, and uncle Luccio should all have NORK tattooed on their forehead. Like a Dr. Seuss character. Oh look, it's a Nork Lork. It's spelled NEWARK, but they say it N-O-R-K. There are too many addresses, people, and detailed memories embedded in my uncles, aunts, parents, and cousins to dive into without honestly boring you to tears, and not because the memories are boring, but because they aren't mine. They belong to the generation who raised me and beyond, so for the lines to suitably capture your attention, one of them would have to write this chapter. Instead, I will highlight the things about Newark that made me listen and feel something in my bones.

My Grandma Yola's rental house in Newark had two bedrooms. The one closer to the front of the house and off the kitchen to the left was the larger of the two, and it's where she'd set up space for my brother and I when we were very young and slept over. She had this enormous closet that was aluminum, almost like lockers, but not hard metal. It had two handles in the middle and a space for a key when locked. Inside these tinny doors were her fur coats. It smelled like moth balls inside, one of the more popular smells of my childhood, signaling the presence of highly meticulous women who liked clothing of all kinds. Hangers covered in silk were the only ones you'd find in these closets, unless it had to hold a ten-pound coat made of fox or mink. They all took immense care in their clothing and belongings, having survived the depression only decades before. Every item counted. Every possession had a pulse.

Grandma Jo lived in a high-rise apartment on Mt. Prospect Avenue in Newark, and what I remember vividly was how hot that apartment got when the sun shone in. She lived way up high. And only three miles from my Grandma Yola in the 1980s. Her two sister-in-laws, Lee and Marie, also lived in that building, and what I remember clearly about Marie was her painted toenails the color of poppies sticking out of her shiny golden slippers. Her toenails were thick, and her toes crooked, but she painted them like a lady. She always smiled at us. And I always got the feeling we could stay as long as we wished. Like she was so happy to see the generation behind her in her building. Which is so stinking Italian.

In Newark, my nose, my fingertips, my tongue, and my eyes were happy. I smelled Grandma's scrambled eggs, the oregano in her Sunday sauce, and the old wood in the kitchen.

In Newark, my aunt Norma lived in a house with a backyard full of marbles in the cement—shaped into numbers and floral patterns. I'd run my fingertips across those designs, imagining the origin and narrative of their placement.

In Newark, my Grandma Yola walked us to and from Prosperity Italian Market for fresh mozzarella balls, our choice of candy, and sometimes a loaf of Italian bread.

In Newark, we'd shop in stores jam-packed with bolts of fabric, piles of slippers, racks of housedresses, and counters overtaken by earrings.

In Newark, my Grandma Yola made us the butteriest wagon-wheel pasta. Grandma Jo, a bowl of elbow macaroni with peas and garlic.

In Newark, my father worked the midnight shifts at PSE&G, commuting from our house down the shore for many years.

In Newark, my eyes lit up at the sound of both my grandma's voices. At the sound of their pans sizzling. At the touch of their fingertips to our arms.

Living in Small Spaces

At a very young age, I developed a love for apartment buildings and the idea of being as cozy as possible in a living space. Our house on Mulberry Place was warm and cozy for sure, and certainly we were toppling all over each other with one full bathroom and a tight half bath downstairs, but it still wasn't "living in a tree like picture book animals" cozy. While on the bus to and from school, I'd daydream about getting off at the apartment building stops with my friends who lived there. I know now that maybe they felt this way about the stops for the neighborhood houses. We all had homes. We all had a unique kind of family. But the space and provisions were different.

I didn't think about those provisions at age five, six, and seven. Only cozy. I loved the idea of apartment living because I imagined it to be like a sort of village or special neighborly thing. I imagined it as a super safe place where my parents and brother were closer in proximity, and our dinners were eaten on the couch instead of a small kitchen. Or if we did have a kitchen, perhaps it was more of a card table, some folding chairs, and we'd be as happy as could be.

My Grandma Jo had moved from Newark into the Bay Berry Apartments in Scotch Plains, New Jersey in the late '80s, and I loved that place. I loved the way the wood floors smelled, and when she'd make a Sunday dinner, the smell permeated every inch of the wooden-centric space. As if the floorboards soaked it in saying, "Yes. More of that, please." The whole apartment felt designed specifically for good cooks—their rich sauces and garlic meant to permanently scar the walls and sheetrock for decades.

Often, my parents would leave me overnight for one or two nights, and that tomato sauce would perfume her apartment for those days until I left. Garlic, tomatoes, oregano, and braciola. It became the smell I'd love forever. Even now when I sauté anything in olive oil, I dream about that apartment and those Sunday visits. But my current open plan house isn't tight enough to saturate the air completely the way Bay Berry Gardens took it in, like a sponge. I'd sleep in my Gram's family room on the couch sofa. That apartment had one bedroom, a kitchen, a bathroom, and her family room. It was one of my favorite small spaces on Earth.

I remember sleeping on the pullout sofa, and sometimes she'd join me if I was nervous or anxious about sleeping away from home. One night, rather than pulling on my Raggedy Ann doll's red stringy hair, I took a fistful of my grandma's scratchy blonde hair. She laughed, though it startled her. She was so lovely and made me feel so safe all the time.

My adoration of cozy spaces explains why I really wanted to live in my old metal Radio Flyer wagon in the summer months. A pillow, my art supplies, and food and water. Right on the side of our house on Mulberry Place under the slowly maturing dogwood for shade. My dad never let me sleep the night out there. I'd beg often, with no success. I wanted to be pressed into my wagon where my legs only hung over a little bit, and with a beach towel and my pillow I'd create a perfectly acceptable bedroom for a night or two. I wanted to live in the space of the grass, moon, stars, and tree shadows in the middle of July. Something about it felt ... independent.

Since my parents objected to me sleeping in that wagon under the dogwood, I settled for eating my lunch and my dessert out there, so I got a taste of pre- and post-sunset skies. I used to imagine it was snowing too, and I was safe in my cozy Radio Flyer, a sort of neighborhood treasure, but also a house all my own. With no roof and a major tendency to rust. My dad scooped up this wagon at a flea market, as it wasn't the new plastic model. I was probably the third or fourth owner, from the looks of it. He was all about the nostalgic brands for toys, vehicles that weren't cars, and gumball machines of varying shape and color.

Sometimes my mom would give me a bag of a dozen corn ears to shuck outside, so I'd take it to the wagon and be truly content for thirty minutes. The silk of the corn husks and strings—the smoothing over of the kernels once it was naked—all extremely balancing for my sensory stuff. My hands and arms would smell of corn husks, and I was flowing in that kind of summer peace until the day the school bus showed up. It felt like I was born for those outdoor chores in my wagon.

I still fantasize about simpler dwellings in my adult life, until of course, someone brings home a stomach bug. Or until we go away on vacation with our two children and trip over each other's feet and words. When you need the space, then it becomes important. In daydreams, it's wonderful to be in close quarters.

One of my biggest fantasies as a kid, and I'm not going to lie—still a little bit now when I visit Lowes or Home Depot—is the sheds in the parking lot. The ones for sale. When I need to be alone, I imagine setting up house and moving in to one of the sheds. Preferably, I'd like it set up in my backyard so that I am both close and semi-accessible to my family, but what a million-dollar business idea to have a parking lot full of quiet sheds. Sanitized after each use. Twenty-four-hour limit. A bed, books, a small TV, and silence. Encased in your own cocoon when you need it. Bring your own food, drinks, a nice padlock on the door. You can use the indoor bathroom that they'll cleverly design with locks on stalls too—also sanitized to the high heavens after each person.

You think I'm kidding. Humans like to be cozy. Some of us love to be alone and hibernate or read for hours. Fresh air is a need. Maybe the sheds are painted in beautiful grays, pale pinks, greens, and blues, and you can reserve the color that best matches your energy.

I'll meet you there at midnight. I'll be in the hunter green shed. Or any green shed. With my markers, my gallon of water, some peanut butter, and a stack of books. I should probably bring a flashlight too.

Nectarine Pits

Things that can pose as art and garbage, depending on the onlooker, are everywhere. Like nectarine pits. I know some people call them stones. That's poetic. I grew up calling them pits. The nectarine pit is ripe (ha) with art. Lines, curves, embroidery of its own. Kind of looks like a brain or a map of a place that's enigmatic and rare. The pit is complex and not pretty. Not like its covering. Think about it—an imperfect swirl burnt in oranges, reds, and yellows. Leading to a hardened brown ... brain?

We always had fruit to eat in my house on the Jersey Shore growing up. My mom would buy them at various farmsteads dotting the highways—I wish I remembered the exact names of them. The peaches, plums, and nectarines were always in abundance. They'd stumble out of her paper bags like active members of the summer family in my house on Mulberry Place in Toms River.

The ones with the most lessons were the nectarines. The ones my mom kept highly stocked from May through early September, and I suppose it was sort of good they went away for a bit and out of season. It made their reappearance that much more special. There were August days where I could easily consume two nectarines and two plums in one day. I was a fruit-loving kid who couldn't wait to stab my teeth into a vitamin-heavy piece of earth. It was like eating the earth itself, I used to pretend. The Garden State's gifts.

In the process of slurping up the nectarine it was my goal to remove every strand and thread of fruit flesh from the erotic brown pit to be left with the most perfectly dried and carved remnant of my textural joy. The pit represented genesis, like an artifact from the first of us. And I imagined keeping each one in a jar collection on a windowsill, only to be told to throw it out before we got ants. "We'll get ants! Ants like sugar!" My mom's one of many childhood proclamations. So I'd often bury that pit in the yard, praying for some nectarine trees to grow on Mulberry Place.

I dreamed that when I buried it deep in Ortley beach's sand under my feet that it lived for decades, and then imagined finding it survived after mounds and pounds of erosion and natural environmental shifts on the shore. Ortley beach's sand and my nectarine pits were indiscernible. Like cracked pepper and salt all blended together furiously.

That cleaned-out nectarine pit left strands of fruit in my teeth for days sometimes. But those perfect cavernous striations. And mazes. What was it? What was the fascination? Was it primal? Was it the layers and twists like a tree trunk, each original, each with a special story. Was it the resemblance to a vagina? I remember sitting on the edge of my bed around the age of nine and bending my head as far as it would go to examine the layers and the skin that made up *my* pit. Where was this hole, exactly? Why does it all feel so fragile, but like at the same time so malleable and twisty?

Eating a nectarine on Ortley beach was a prelude to the day ahead full of oily sunshine dreams and my mom pushing grapes and lots of water in our direction—from the same red jug of icy water that we'd all share. I smelled their cigarette breath on the mouthpiece. But it didn't bother me. It was family. The nectarines sweetened the smoke.

My mom would choose the most round and plump nectarines from the Jersey Fresh markets, and it occurred to me even that young, that there had to have been some kind of god for fruit like nectarines to grow in the world. Saint Pulp? The first slice *or bite* is heartbreaking—watching the perfection break apart for my own pleasure. Watching the devastation of the whole for its pieces.

Sometimes when it was not quite ripe enough, I'd break the nectarine in half, rather than bite it. When the nectarine cracks open cleanly, there's a crunch. Or more like a poof.

There's this amazing oval truth to the pit. Cavernous truth—I'd suck, eat and daydream about the dates the golden-skinned girl would go on with her hunky boyfriend. I'd watch them run up and down Ortley's wet sand on the edge of the ocean. They'd spend all day covered in coconut oil on the beach, go home, shower, then meet up at the Southern House for chicken and ribs with their families. Journey or Foreigner would play on the car radio. That was the Ortley fantasy. Which purse would she pair with her denim and hot pink lips? Would she go with the dangly earrings, or the yellow triangles?

The Ortley couple and the fruit drippings down my throat so sunshiny sweet and full of hope. I'd daydream about being a teenager.

Maybe the nectarine experience, the digging down to the pit with voracity, was the antidote to the secondhand smoke clouding our kitchen on Mulberry Place. Or maybe that fleshy fruit exploration would erase the trauma of the awful nuns yelling at us during CCD Wednesdays? Or the cure for not being brave enough to jump into a back handstand. The physics I couldn't find within me. Maybe the nectarine feast would answer why John across the street wouldn't kiss a tomboy like me. Or maybe my tongue hitting the pit in victory would replace the never-won victory of my mom saying *yes* to me sleeping in the wagon in front of the house under the medium sized oak tree.

Maybe the nectarine bliss was the antithesis of death.

Maybe nectarines are just peaches in drag. Smooth. Magnificent.

Maybe the nectarine pits are mirrors to a perfect world of fruit that grows in the Ortley Beach sun. And ripens for our pleasure, and since humans have a lot of rotten things to endure during our journey, fruits and pits so mystical like the nectarines exist for our adoration. Tongue through the grooves at the end while we reflect on the nourishment. We're so lucky.

If you google Nectarine Lane you'll find it in Liverpool, New York. Liverpool is a small village in Onondaga New York—a suburb of Syracuse. One day I will drive to Nectarine Lane purely to find out that nothing about that road or street feels very nectariney. (It's surrounded by Blueberry Road and Kumquat Lane.) Maybe the Purple Pie Man visits on Halloween. That's a timely reference and I pray some of you laugh, even a soft chuckle.

Nectarines dot the New Jersey produce sections of farmers markets each summer with the vibrance of a Beach Boys song. Nectarines were one of the many fruits I was obsessed with and truly in awe of from a very young age. Next in line—strawberries, then plums, then probably watermelon. All from our glorious farm stands dotting the Jersey Shore.

Because ... Science

When I was a child, I thought everyone developed a headache on Sundays in the backseat of their parents' car, especially if the sky was a beaming block of sunshine, or if it was rainy and humid. I thought everyone felt tired after a day of people's voices and environmental mish-mosh. I was wrong. People can make it through those car rides with the sun on their face and window closed, very cheerfully, it turns out. Turns out people can also enjoy holiday shopping in department stores without breaking into a cold sweat.

As a kid, and throughout most of my life, I've been experiencing what scientists sometimes call a "sensory minefield." As an adult, it occurs to me that all my experiences in life would have been different if that minefield were absent. Truthfully, would they have been incrementally more satisfying experiences? I'm thinking it depends on the scenario. Like perhaps I wouldn't have been so nauseated in church, or maybe I'd have been able to be in a car with all my teammates without getting a massive headache before the game because of their voices for an hour, in my face.

Sensory defensiveness is not the main problem. It's the symptoms that happen with it—tension in the body, anxiety down the legs, and often, anger or frustration. So, it's not that getting sick in the backseat is where it would end. The tightness in my shoulders all day long afterward, and the stress of that lingering carsickness would permeate the rest of my day. The nervous system is complex—wires and braids and twists and turns in every possible direction, so of course, I've felt "a mess" after a day spent in a huge conference room with guest speakers, other attendees, sugary doughnuts on my plate, and the heat jacked up to eighty-five degrees. The recovery from a day like this is about twenty-four to forty-eight hours. I lived/live at the mercy of my nervous system, but it's gotten better with age and awareness. Sometimes the solution is as simple as my thick wavy locks thrown up in a bun, off my neck, a giant glass of ice water, and an arduous, uphill walk. Other times, the only cure is a good night's sleep. According to science, sensory affective processing disorders are rarely outgrown. But fear not, accommodations, products like weighted blankets and cooling pillowcases, are always being invented and improved. And praise goddess, not many people in my circles wear perfume anymore.

Humans have a biochemistry that requires balancing, and the items being balanced are: serotonin, adrenaline, and the nervous system as a whole. When these items are out of whack, so can the individual be. Lord knows mine has been out of whack at varying levels at various times in my life to the point of fear. Through talk therapy, Reiki therapy, and a low dose of Lexapro, I manage it well. Finally. It took a long time. There are times I am overloaded, and times I am under-loaded, if you can visualize that. When I first read this, I imagined a plate of food, like linguini with clams. That plate is terrible when it's too full or when it's teeny tiny like those chic places in Brooklyn where you leave hungry and inhale two slices of pizza an hour later.

I learned that my sensory processing disorder loves to pop up in the passenger seat too, much to the driver's utter dismay. If I'm not driving, I think we're driving too fast, too close, and a crash is coming. It's right around the corner. I can't feel the reality of the motion. It's perceived differently than non-affected passengers. It's a good time. I swear. Gripping the door frame, hanging on for dear life anytime the driver exceeds sixty-five miles per hour is a joyride.

The next time someone is telling you you're high maintenance, fussy, or picky, show them the science. You're not any of those things. It's real, and it's not hopeless. Listen to children when they let you know their environment is in their way. When they tell you that the woman's strong perfume is bothering them, consider valuing their words before they vomit or get a migraine. And biggest of all, roll down that window if they kindly ask. Our ideal temperature is not necessarily your ideal temperature, and again—unless you want them to throw up or have a full out panic attack, consider their needs.

Yuletide Segments

I grew up in the kind of Italian-American household where Christmas was spread over two full days, existing in subsections, marked by towns and dotted by food. All the food. It was super exciting for a nineteen-year-old with an enormous appetite. In our family, Christmas Eve was the *high priestess.* My mom, Corinna, was the Queen of Wands. And by queen, I mean *we* were the ant colony who fulfilled tasks as she buzzed them through her mandible, in no logical order and with no manners. "Move this. Set that. Clean those!"

To the queen's credit, it was a stressful preparation in a house of Italian zig-zagging. Tablecloths to be ironed, fennel to be sliced, olives to be drained then plated, fish to be cleaned, crabs boiled, and the list would repeat, reverse, and twist back into itself. "John! Grab me some pans from the laundry room shelf! Elaina, fold the cloth napkins for the table. JP, wipe the counter."

We were a well olive-oiled machine led by a very southern Italian Scorpio matriarch with gold specks in her eyes—lined with passion, fire, and sometimes agitation. One never truly knew how to distinguish one from the other two. When someone discovers the best detection method, you can e-mail me. In the meantime, allow my sensory journey of a two-day endless celebration/battlefield entertain you.

My mom created a setup in our Mulberry Place garage to cook flounder. Her electric fry pans sizzled on a wobbly folding table—the fish already egged and floured. "I don't want to stink up the house." The fish was always for one of two things—a Friday when we *maybe* observed the "no meat Fridays," or Christmas Eve dinner. Southern Italian tradition is about abstaining from meat on the Eve of Christmas—it's actually called Feast of the Seven Fishes. In southern Italy it's known as La Vigilia to signify the vigilance. Traditionally, Italians throughout history would enjoy shrimp, octopus, bacalao, clam, crab, anchovies, and more.

Secretly, the stinky fishy smell signaled a deep vibration of Christmas madness within me, knowing my two first-cousins, Marc and Peter would be at our house in a few hours, ready to laugh at things we laughed at together, twice a year. Maybe three. We laughed at the patterns of our parents' words, the endearing nature of my grandmother and her sister, and anything else that seemed ... dramatic, in the key of Italian vowels. That fried fish smell remains one of the most triggering (in the best way) smells for me. "Where's the party? Who's coming over? How can I perform a dance or monologue for them?"

Even though the frying of the flounder was conducted in our small garage off the laundry room, the smell drifted into the house faintly, letting us all know, that it was indeed, Christmas Eve. Christmas Eve meant cousins from Cranford, my aunt Rose, my uncle Luccio and his gigantic VHS camcorder, tangled voices, my grandmother's dominant, but delicate presence, and gifts stacked in the living room.

The fried flounder was mostly for the adults in the room, yet very recently my cousin Marc told me that he loved it too.

Not me. Back then the odor of fish repulsed me. The thought of putting any fish in my mouth, because of its smell, made me gag. Palates change as we mature. The kids only ate the linguini with a dab of butter, fresh parsley, salt, and pepper. My mom had lots of separate plates for separate preferences. My aunt Norma brought her own lettuce leaves in small margarine tubs: fluffy green leaf or butter variety. My mom prepared a huge pot of clams, shrimp, sometimes crabmeat, and salty white fish called bacalao that made me dry heave more than the flounder. It was like scooping a spoonful of the Atlantic Ocean into your mouth ... at low tide. Ok, I lied earlier. Bacalao bothered me. Spears of cucumber, black olives, raw fennel, all for hand-picking before, during, and after our meal.

A soundtrack pierced the air from very early the morning of Christmas Eve, starring Johnny Mathis. My personal favorite was *A Partridge Family Christmas.* We originally played the vinyl version, but as the years grew from early 1980s to late 1980s and early 1990s, we had the full cassette, then the CD. My parents owned the cabinet unit kind of stereo that included two four-foot speakers in our formal living room, and I'll fight you to the death if you claim any streamlined, tiny contemporary speakers are better. Cue Johnny swooning so delightfully about Farmer Gray and the perfect ending to a perfect day. Usually somewhere right before my uncle Luccio, my mom's oldest brother, would arrive with my aunt Rose and two cousins, my dad would switch the music selection to the local radio station of the Jersey Shore, which still lives and breathes—92.7 WOBM FM. They'd play Christmas tunes all day with quick weather updates. I think my dad assumed it would feel more genuine to be surprised with each holiday hit taking its turn playing in a random mix.

Right around one I'd get so excited. No matter my age. I only saw my Cranford family a few times a year, so I enjoyed their time at our house. It was a chance to see the sibling dynamic between Luccio and my mom and just how different they were, yet secretly, how alike. How they looked so much like our grandfather who died many years before he got to see any of his grandchildren, or even meet my father. If you look at my mom's hands and my Uncle Luccio's hands, you see their genetic bond. Their hands in conversation and expression are even more fascinating. My cousins, brother, and I saw it, commented on it, and relished the bond.

Then my very much alive grandmother would arrive with her even more alive sister Norma in tow with my mom's youngest brother, Uncle Frankie, and his brood from the west side of New York City. I wish I could put a QR code right about here with a link to my home videos of this Christmas Eve noise. The festive nature, and the competing Italian-American voices tossing themselves all over my fried-flounder-scented house on Mulberry Place. My parents left Essex County, Jersey behind when I turned about two years old. They wanted beach and salt air. I am grateful, yet the Cranford-Westfield portion of the state forever occupies a lot of love in my heart. Both sides of my family still live there, so I have a reason to visit.

Grandma Yola and Aunt Norma were forces of an Italian nature. Their own dialect, their own energy, and widows for decades who could take care of themselves, but for having a driver's license. "Oh we walk everywhere in Nutley." If you dare even imply to any of the women in my family that they are helpless or dependent, you'll get a salty earful. Christmas Eve was never ever the same once they both died—Norma first at age ninety-five, then Yola a good decade later at ninety-eight.

Grandma Yola and Aunt Norma were fussy about food. And chocolate, clothing, carpets, shoes, bath towels, skincare, and hair.

My grandmother brought a few pieces of her good chocolate, only for my mom to remind her that the chocolate she served was "good" too. Aunt Norma would sometimes also sneak in a container of cooked macaroni brought from her kitchen, probably a cup measured out. They were both teeny tiny women who "watched their weight" and ate like royalty from the curated selection of their own making. Tons of greens, a protein like lamb or veal, and a starch. They made the food, from start to finish on an average non-Christmas day in their Nutley Senior Building, and then they ate their food. "Corinna it all is delicious," they'd comment. They meant it, and they ate it, so maybe their own containers were more a statement than anything else. If they were to indulge in a sweet, it had to be chosen from brand names with their stamps of approval. Otherwise, you'd get the stink-eye, and you'd sort of feel like crap for not being so particular about what you put into your own body. I loved them for it though. We all did. They were the highlights of our family on those holiday occasions. Mostly because Christmas Eve dinner chatter would spotlight them and the infamous archives of the shoe-shopping expeditions that took place a couple times a year at the Willow Brook Mall.

December meant calf-length, wool, button-down coats with collars for Yola and Norma. Yola sported the violet purple and Norma dazzled in fuchsia, both jewel-toned to match their matching jewel-toned silk scarves worn over their hair, just as you'd imagine. Think modern-day Strega Nona. These are critical details because the un-coating and de-scarving process was step one in the entertainment they'd provide us, and knowingly. "Oh Madonn, it's cold out!" "Oh Madonn, don't put my coat on a bed. Hang it up, please. Thank you, Elaina!" "Oh, Elaina, not like that. Don't wrinkle the arms."

We'd hang out in conversation between the kitchen, living room, and tiny TV den that lead into the kitchen. Or whatever variation our house was situated in that particular year—my mom liked to change up our rooms, always seeking to maximize the space in our basement-less home. An average of three conversations would burst through the walls, simultaneously, as Italians naturally allow and can't help but create. My father would share his nostalgic toy or techy catalogue with my cousin Pete, and I'd usually find something to talk to Marc about—we were kindred spirits in a certain take-me-or-leave-me way. Pete and I would chat up our latest musical diets and bands—what concerts we were excited about, local indie stuff. My brother would skate around the conversations, way more interested in sports and his own friends, who would show up a few hours later for dessert. The four of us clicked just enough to be comfortable and happy together for this day of the year when probably, as teens, we wanted to be talking to our friends.

When I was much younger, in say third grade, I'd prepare Christmas showcases for all four of us to perform for the adults, i.e. the entire script of *A Charlie Brown Christmas.* I had it all prepared from who would read which part to fake snow and trees. Those plays never happened, as Christmas Eve in an extremely fussy Italian home is not the arena to showcase a kid's creative spirit randomly. No offense to any of the adults I speak about—it was a different climate at Christmas, and the traditions won. Other cake and coffee nights with family friends proved to be my chance to dance and lip sync.

I don't remember my mom being big on the before-dinner "pickers" as we like to call them on the Battista side. She didn't want everyone filling up before she presented her feast. The feast required maximum appetite—a salad the size of Alaska, fresh Italian bread, the fishes mentioned above in various forms, clams oregenata, chicken cutlets for the non-fish eaters, and whatever midwestern cold bean salad my aunt Sheila (a Midwesterner) brought. That bean salad sat all alone in her bowl, year after year, and she had herself a merry little Christmas while the rest of the dishes were wiped clean. My uncle Luccio recently coined the best term for my mom's Christmas Eve spread: an art museum of food. It was pure art, honestly. From the bowls she used to the variety and amount she cooked. Nothing was overly formal about the dishware once I got older, but in the early '80s my mom broke out her Noritake black-and-white Chinaware—a wedding gift from her 1972 wish list.

The tablescape was very authentically Ricci. What does that mean, exactly? It meant: a hunter green cloth tablecloth with various woven basket trivets, stainless steel slotted spoons for serving, cloth napkins usually maroon or the same green as the tablecloths. The pasta bowls were wide and round, not deep. Since our crowd was large, and it included a child component, my dad added a folding table somewhere in the mix covered in the same vinyl tablecloth that I now own—white with pine trees, holly berries, and pinecones.

My mom kept her apron on until she sat down to eat. My aunts helped, and I tried to be a good Italian girl, but I was much more in tune to the conversations my dad, cousins, uncles were having. Yes, I was kind of a bad Italian girl in the eyes of the patriarchy. What can I say? I was born a very protesting,

Aquarian archetype. Without realizing it, I was establishing my voice even then. As in, okay, I know everyone thinks I should be in the kitchen helping to scrub, wipe, and dry the dinnerware smeared with red sauce and olive oil, but I'd rather be at the table with my uncles defending Madonna's presence in the world or discussing how I am going to be a professional creative person someday.

I didn't say those words to the women in the kitchen, but maybe they knew by my actions. And it's not that I didn't help at all. It's that I wasn't a key player in that process, so I didn't push the issue. They appeared to have it covered, so why screw with their system? My uncle's stepdaughter loved being near my mom and asking her if she'd die a forty-year-old virgin, so I backed off. I let her load the dishwasher and dry the bowls so that she had my mom's full attention for inquiries about things I didn't care about. "Aunt Corinna, I go places. I join events. Nobody notices me."

Back at the empty table, over a glass of wine for him and iced tea for me, my uncle Frankie made sure I knew what a career entailed: "You know Elaina. It's not that simple to become an executive in advertising." Italian-American families have black cloud tendencies, you see. Why I should do this or that, and even then, it wasn't always a road to success. Uncle Luccio talked about his job in accounting for customs and the many ports of Newark. He leaned more towards the sunshine than my uncle Frankie, so I listened to his memories more than Uncle Frankie's dark cloud advice.

My mom was always being my mom: "Ma, you can eat something with salt on it once in a while." She was not the "Yes mom" kind of daughter, and neither am I. Neither will my girls be. That's how we like it, and that's how we play tug-o-war with ourselves: Be a free-thinking and independent woman, but also love your mother.

My cousins, brother, and I thought we knew it all from year to year—"Oh my God, what are the adults talking about now? They're so ancient." We were entirely Gen X before we had a name. As if we'd seen the truth at age fourteen.

Once dinner and its multiple conversations were devoured it was about an hour before six o'clock Mass at our local parish, St. Joseph's. We'd attend a very hot and crowded Mass and get out right before my sinuses did their protest march and make it home alive and in the dark suburban night for gifts and dessert. We were on hour number five at this point. I would feel the exhaustion creeping in. Adrenaline always won though. This was where my mom would say—"You're exhausted? I'm the one doing all the work!" She was right that she was physically doing all of the work, but my nervous system was on overload. I was overjoyed, but as a sensory kid who felt dysregulated, that also meant I was drained. I remember taking a beat to sit down on the sofa next to my grandma while she held my hand, a chance for me to reconnect with myself and breathe. I didn't know I was doing it on purpose. I know it now.

Gift-giving was my favorite part at all ages. When I was young it was my favorite for obvious reasons. Did my aunt Rose buy me a pocketbook that reminded her of me? Beside the ten-dollar bill in the bank envelope, did my mom guide my grandmother to the earrings I saw for five dollars at Foxmoor or Deb? Then there was my uncle Frankie. If you read my first book, you'd know that his gifts were the puzzling, yet unique ones. A flashlight pen of my favorite color green or a window herb garden that I'd never plant because not once did I express an interest in gardening or green thumbing. Though I did like the mystery of his gifts. In the older days, my cousins, brother, and I received brand new winter coats, in which we'd put them on and model them for the cameras. As we opened our gifts, one at a time to the tune of "To Aunt Sheila, from Elaina and JP. To Corinna, from Marc and Peter," Uncle Luccio would film the entire fiasco of torn wrapping paper, tumbling boxes, and anxious kids waiting for their names to be called. "Elaina had all checks, no Xs," my uncle Frankie would announce. He said he kept track of all of us all year. One year all four of us got sweatshirts with the name Ricci on them because apparently it was a brand of Italian food too. There's a photo somewhere of us modeling the sweatshirt I'd never wear in public at the age of fourteen. I never said anything back then, but my rebel heart protested the gesture a little bit because I was technically a Battista by name. I played along with a smile because I wasn't taught to protest something like that. It was the thought that counted.

After gift opening, my dad would make sure not a triangle or teardrop of paper remained, and that all of the debris was safely secured in a Hefty bag and already put out to the garbage can on the side of our house. My mom, aunts, grandmothers, and step-cousins would place the nut and fruit baskets on the dining room table to prep our appetites for dessert. Italians don't rush a meal. Italians like their pears, nuts, wine, and figs prior to the big, sweet finish. During nuts and fruit, we'd continue to reflect on the comedy of Yola and Norma because they were always ready to be the stars of the show. My mom would pour tiny amounts of wine from the ceramic fruit decanter that once belonged to my dad's grandmother. We drank our wine from short juice glasses. We didn't use stem wine glasses. Or if we did, I don't remember them the way I do the juice glasses with a trickle of red or white during nuts and fruit. At some point over the years of hosting Christmas Eve, I'm sure my mom whipped out her stemware, but overall, our style was more laid back.

The last portion of Christmas Eve was the serving of dessert. You'd think no one had room or steam left to enjoy, imbibe, slurp, all of it, but we did. Our bodies year after year must've known how to pace themselves even if our minds were unaware of the cogs and wheels behind it.

I don't descend from women who excel in baking. Not even the Italian cookies you're dreaming of as you read this. Dessert was the simplest part of my mom's museum of food. She'd make what I thought were the best chocolate chip cookies—crispy and firm, with still a hint of chewy. My aunt Rose often brought her homemade pizzelles. A box of "good" chocolate would be the centerpiece, and then maybe some kind of plain Bundt cake. Dessert wasn't opulent, but it finished the day with a soft Christmas ping.

Usually a few of my brothers' friends from the neighborhood would stop by right around dessert time, and they'd blend in well and mostly listen to the chatty Italians around the table. Or they'd be hammered with questions by said Italians. "Hey Chris. Did your mom make six entrees too?" "Hey Mike. Eat more cookies!" They were not Italian, so this was a special carnival for them to attend after their quiet meals with their own non-Italian families.

When it was time to say goodbye to the two entourages—the Cranford and the NYC/Nutley components, it was never swift, nor tidy. It was chaotic, loud, cacophonous, and true to the nature of our emotionally charged heritage. "Oh, you're leaving? This was a nice time ... here don't forget your leftovers. Ma, I won't eat all this, have it for lunch over the weekend. Luna, where's my scarf? Marc did you use the bathroom, we have a long ride! Frankie, don't forget to give me the name of that brand of pasta. Norma, do you have your pills?" The Cranford crew was off to their next destination in southern Jersey near the Delaware border, and my uncle Frankie had to bring the sassy Nutley ladies to the city with him for the night stayover into Christmas Day. For the Battista host component, we had crumbs on the carpet and tablecloth puddles to deal with, along with getting organized for the second segment of Christmas. It was nonstop protocol—one we anticipated and practiced year after bayberry candlelit year.

Christmas morning resembled an enormous hangover. Our stomachs full of pasta and fish and pounds of my mom's chocolate chip cookies. Throw in random pieces of wrapped Italian chocolate, and you've got four people with bellies screaming over sugar and temporarily addicted to the feeling of full. We'd open our gifts in a Christmas-drunkenness, enjoy some scrambled eggs, Taylor ham, and tater tots, then get ready for the next segment of our Christmas: Christmas Day at Aunt Connie and Uncle Bob's house in Westfield, New Jersey. The morning wasn't complete though, until we called Aunt Connie and Uncle Bob on the phone during breakfast—my mom reiterating that she'd bring her famous cream puffs or a side of roasted peppers. Sometimes both. Aunt Connie would tell my dad how busy their gift shop, The Arrangement, was on Christmas Eve with all of the last-minute shoppers. We'd shower, throw on our new duds, perfume, or cologne, and leave around two—straight up the Garden State Parkway North to Exit 135.

Part II: Westfield, NJ

On the way up the parkway, we'd predict as a quartet how the day would unfold at my aunt Connie and uncle Bob's house in Westfield, the town right next to Cranford where their gift shop thrived. The same Cranford where Luccio lived. Toms River is Exit 82 on the Garden State Parkway, while Westfield sits at exit 135. An exact hour, door to door. New Jerseyans survive on this unit of measurement known as the Exit.

Predictions about Christmas Day included how much my uncle Tony, my dad's younger brother by sixteen years, would make fun of my dad or playfully imitate my aunt, uncle, cousins, or his mother, my Grandma Jo. He was the funny uncle, and they referred to him as Buster Ball when he was younger. Other aliases included Screw Ball and Antny. We'd predict how much food would be on the table and whether my uncle Bob would cry out of sentiment for a gift he might receive from their best friends, Ed and Barbara, also the co-owners of The Arrangement. We'd compete for the biggest laugh on that car ride, and before we knew it, we'd arrive at my aunt's house ready for an extended day poring over food, family, laughter, and gifts. Christmas Day, like Christmas Eve, had very distinct segments.

Segment One: My very exhausted aunt Connie, in her pencil skirt, sweater, pantyhose, and slippers would put out delightful plates of afternoon appetizers. She'd skip her contacts and sport her glasses on Christmas after a chaotic and nonstop week of examining item labels and price tags at the store. The sun shone through the picture window of their downstairs living room—my grandmother sat next to my dad on the white sofa, and my brother, mother, uncle Tony and his family scattered about. I liked the floor, but it was sort of early in the day for that, so I'd squish in on the sofa too, vying for the spot next to Grandma Jo. She smelled like pink roses. I'd find my place on the carpet later when my shoes were off and my belly ached, full of Christmas food. The appetizers were usually tightly rolled salami slices, chunks of provolone, fresh mozzarella, and some kind of breadstick. Sometimes the cold cuts wrapped around the breadstick. Some years, she tooth-picked cantaloupe. Marinated mushrooms and artichokes peppered the plate other years. We'd all catch up on our lives during "pickers." My uncle Tony would bust my dad's chops about something, often work at PSE&G where they were both employed, along with Uncle Bob. It was a family affair, PSE&G, or Public Service, as my dad preferred. Johnny Mathis and Perry Como songs cascaded from the old-fashioned radio my aunt and uncle had hidden in the bottom of a wooden cabinet near their carpeted stairs that led to the master bedroom and bathroom. More guests would arrive—their best friends and co-owners, their best friend's daughter Alyson, Uncle Bob's sister Cathy and mom Lucy. We'd eat, talk, and prime ourselves for the Christmas Dinner simmering in their small kitchen.

Segment Two: Our Christmas Dinner was fairly traditional for an Italian-American family—a starter of my mom's lasagna, maybe even my aunt's, depending on how they divvied the duties each year. Then a roasted turkey, a baked ham, and many beautifully brown-edged side dishes like potatoes with breadcrumbs and cheese. My aunt overcooked her broccoli (I didn't realize it was overcooked until I was much older), fresh bread, and a salad of sorts. The din of the hour, tinny and wide, was made up of silverware against plates, voices, Johnny's songs faint in the background telling us about chestnuts and Farmer Gray. Usually, we'd all find something funny to obsess over and get my grandmother in a silly headspace, where she'd laugh and her shoulders would bounce in between her bites and swallows. Uncle Tony led that laughter brigade, in which he'd usually bring up a goofy memory like my dad playing his trusty accordion as a little kid. My uncle called him a dweeb for it. Since my dad was my grandmother's unspoken favorite, she'd say, "Anthony, he was very good at the accordion." He'd then imitate the accordion action, arms opened and closed, getting my brother and me to roar in laughter, thus making Grandma Jo chuckle even harder. It was contagious and lovely. Grandma Josephine was more than an angel with her blonde Betty White hair and her silk blouses, usually involving a low hanging bow on the collar portion. She was a good sport and a soothing grandmother three hundred and sixty-five days a year. She didn't have the vanity about her looks like my Grandma Yola, yet both were equally genuine.

We'd stuff our faces, talk and laugh some more, then roll over to the couch after helping to clear the large oak table in the dining room. When you have a small kitchen, sometimes the less people helping is better. Otherwise, you trip and bump and knock each other over in the clean up space. As mentioned earlier, cleaning up wasn't my forte, so I'd sit with the boys and add my two cents.

The thing about chatting with members of an Italian-American family is the overlap and the cacophony of several conversations happening at once, and the small window of time you have to answer a question. There's a short attention span. It can easily be mistaken for rudeness, poor manners, or hyperactivity. It's mostly the last one. We get excited, we get into it, our mind and emotions race, and our thoughts churn at an unreasonable pace, wanting to relate and connect our own ideas and experience on the topic. My dear friend Ella and I had lunch recently and discussed this. It has its downfalls as you realize that friends interpret these conversational behaviors in negative ways. "Elaina is a lot. She never lets me finish. She gets so hyper." It can be perceived as this but believe me when I say it's a cultural behavior that requires years of practice to correct. Italians are a people driven by emotional fire and a love of conversation. Coming from Christmases where I not only competed to be heard in the crowd, but also competed with loud men, created an adult who has to actively pay attention to when I interrupt my friends. If I've frequently interrupted you—now you know to blame the childhood Christmas gatherings. And Easter. And Thanksgiving. Birthdays. You get the idea. I'm a work in progress.

In between all of it, we'd make our way up or down to their bathrooms as needed. In the blue bathroom upstairs, there was always a cinnamon or vanilla candle lit for the day, and though me and candles weren't the best of friends, to this day, I think of Aunt Connie when anyone has a bathroom candle lit. It does cover the poop smell, let's be honest. With a house full of eaters, perhaps it's necessary to think of these things.

Segment Three: This was our favorite part. We'd all spread out in the living room, just off the dining room where the afternoon had begun only a couple hours earlier. The sun had set, and it was outdoor holiday light time through the picture window on Bell Drive. My brother and I would haul piles of gifts down the stairs from the TV room and arrange them neatly near the loveseat where my very animated uncle Tony would read: "To Aunt Connie, from Corinna and John," and one at a time, we'd open our gifts. We'd then take the time to admire the gift so the recipient felt good about it. It was an embarrassing event, really. Eventually, we'd reached the bottom of the large shiny pile. Silk ribbons barely got a chance to sprinkle the carpet with my dad or aunt waiting with a huge black Hefty bag. The Battistas do not like mess, and as you know from the Christmas Eve portion of the program, my dad headed that operation with ease. Often when my aunt and uncle's best friend Ed would open his gifts, he'd cry over the limited collection Santa figurine that my aunt and uncle bought for him from their own store. I used to think, "Wow. Some men are super emotional." My dad and his brother were not those men. "Oh Connie and Bob," Ed said. "I'm so touched." His wife Barbara with her big round hair and buttoned up blouse would touch her heart and let out a loud laugh of joy.

"Hey Bob. No power tools or toolboxes for you this year?" Uncle Tony would exclaim. We'd all laugh, and then he'd be encouraged to remind us all that Uncle Bob didn't like to repair or build things that way my dad did. I supposed this was his emotional expression of love toward my dad.

Segment Four: This was right about the time that we'd all feel particularly tired and ready to call it a night, but segment four always began right after gifts, close to eight. Dessert was being jostled from containers to serving plates in the kitchen, then shipped to the next room onto the dining room table. Final touches to cakes, cookies piled high in their homemade glory. And the doorbell. My dad's uncle Nick and his family had arrived from their long day either in Staten Island or my cousin Cookie's house in Holmdel. They made the trip because no one holds Christmas Day like my aunt and uncle—candles lit, music kissing the air, and so ... much ... food. My brother and I knew we couldn't ask to go home yet. As much as we wanted to check in with our friends during this era before cell phones. We'd eat dessert with the Staten Island Donadios, laugh some more, eat nuts and fruit too, open more gifts, then collapse in a very full, gassy heap on the couch again.

Segment Six: The concluding segment of the two-day Italian-American food bash was the parkway drive home. My dad in the driver's seat, mom next to him, and my brother and me in the back. You'd think we would be in a stupor. Between the heat in my aunt's house, the over stimulus of voices and food, and the overall yuletide of the past two days. But a crack of the window into the December air woke us up. The reason the cold air was part of the scene was because of the farting. All of us, farting garlic farts and finding it both disgusting and hysterical, caught between the two. Honestly, it was mostly my brother and I doing it from the backseat, and my mom would let out a hearty, "Oh! Roll down the window. That's disgusting!" While simultaneously caught in a deep and meaningful spiral of laughter.

We'd arrive home about eleven, lug the gifts inside, shower, and eat a cheese and rye sandwich. Because eating breeds eating, and we weren't ready to let the holiday go. I'd call my boyfriend of the hour, and eventually we'd all call it a night. Everyone pleased with their gifts. Everyone feeling the love of family. Everyone vowing to not eat like that until next Christmas. My senses would drown into themselves for the following days leading up to New Years. In recovery. On hiatus. I'd survived the over-stimulus, and mostly because of the love, food, and tradition that becomes part of the soul's brain.

* When I first wrote this piece, my uncle Tony was alive. And then he got his diagnosis and grim prognosis. I sent him these pages. They touched his heart. He read them aloud on the phone to my aunt Connie. He passed away September 17, 2023. We all miss him terribly. And Christmastime will never be the same without him. He was an energy that shone brightly.

Tickle My Arm

From what my aunt Connie tells me, arm tickling has been a tradition on the Battista side of the family for as far back as she can recall—back to her Grandma Annie, who is my Great Grandma Annie. The arm tickle originates as a sensation of decompression and an expression of maternal love. Almost like it could be in the last scene of a Disney movie as the solution to the family's problems—the broken curse, cured from an arm tickle. My youngest child loves it, and this is without introducing or prompting it. My oldest can't stand the feeling. Genetic biologists: call me, and we'll chat. Is it a gene? Why does one kid like it and the other doesn't and how did she know about it without a prompt?

Here is what it looks like: You shower. You get your comfy cotton pajamas on, and you settle in for the night. When I was younger, I'd sleep at my aunt's house an hour from my own, and we'd sit upstairs in her small TV room after a hot day outside working the sidewalk sale in Cranford. We worked at her store all day, right in the middle of a bustling Dickensian downtown. We were full from dinner and relaxed from our showers. We'd settle in on the couch, my uncle on one end, my aunt in the middle, and me on the other side of her.

She'd flip her arm, interior side up, and I'd tickle up and down with my nail—it's more of a glide. Now as a lifelong nail biter, she really got the worst end of this deal. After about five minutes, we'd switch. It was a meditation. It is equivalent to maybe a set of deep breathing exercises in which you can wash away the stress of anything in your system, on your mind. An elemental form of decompression. We were able to carry on conversations and watch a show, but really we were melting into the mellow. We were subconsciously focused on how our body just ... unwound. My uncle didn't think we were nuts. It just was our thing. There's likely a part of every human being that responds to touch positively, even if it was during a small portion of their lives—a mother's hand held in yours, a touch of the head, where someone clears away a piece of hair. Those moments when the rest of the world falls away.

°

Grandma Jo (short for Josephine) had rough, worked hands with long fingernails—longer than I was used to on any woman in my family. Sort of wide and rectangular, rather than narrow and elegant. She'd find a portion of my forearm faced up and use all of her fingernails to scoop and lightly scratch. Not too tickly, nor too rough. When I was young, she'd do this on Christmas Day on my aunt's couch during our after-dinner lull and digestive blobbiness. Tired and full. Happy-sleepy. As I got older and I'd visit her on the second floor of her Scotch Plains senior building, I'd sit on the floor in front of her—she'd sit in her mustard gold velvety armchair, and she'd do the same scoop and gentle scratch to my neck under my hair. Want to talk about decompression and a feeling of pure grandmotherly love? I miss those visits. We'd watch Giada make spaghetti or catch reruns of game shows. She'd comment on how big Giada's teeth were. Or how "nice of a fella" the game show host was. I didn't have the heart to tell her that this show was decades old at this point. It didn't matter what we were watching or what we spoke about. It mattered that we were spending time together and she was using her long nails to tickle my neck. Sometimes she'd play with my hair, and I'd fight falling asleep. There is no more relaxing pastime than having your hair played with for a sensory kid/teen/adult like me.

o

Sitting with my Grandma Yola was different than a "tickle my arm" scenario. Firstly, she didn't watch TV until the evening, as a rule. Secondly, she was a spine rubber. She'd find my spine from the lumbar area and do a rub/press up to the cervical and comment, "Madonn, how straight and strong your spine is. God bless you." Again, to a sensory child, I felt at ease, decompressed, and very unraveled by the gesture. Instinctually, she knew I needed this kind of input, and perhaps at some level, so did she. I never asked her. It was pure instinct on her part. Or maybe in her younger years, she liked her back rubbed too. She'd rub my neck because she had sinus issues, and she knew the kind of tension that could build in the human body because of sinus pressure, particularly the shoulders and neck. That's just another theory of how she knew that it felt good. When my first marriage was crumbling, I'd sit with my mom on her couch, my head in her lap, and she'd play with my hair and rub my scalp as we watched TV. I knew all would be okay.

My Grandma Yola liked to wrap up my visits to her Nutley apartment by taking artifacts out to show me at her kitchen table. Anything and everything worth sharing, discussing, enjoying, or contemplating happened at kitchen tables with the women in my family. Sometimes she'd present a box or album of photos of my Grandpa Peter from his boyhood in Italy. Or their exciting New York City nightlife when my mom was growing up in Montclair. My favorite items that she'd routinely pull out came from a three-foot wooden chest she had below a hallway mirror in the area between her kitchen and walkway to the front door. Inside the chest she'd keep important mail, coupons, random saint charms on ribbons, reused boxes that once held chocolates, and maybe a tin or two of coins or non-valuable jewelry. Her stash of gummy bears lived there too.

The item I am building up to is her small storybooks with religious leanings. Picture a chapbook or a thick pamphlet of sorts, watercolor-printed, stapled securely in the middle. The mini books ranged probably from twenty to thirty pages, and they all had titles like *Nature's Blessings, Seasons and Psalm,* or *Ribbons of Love.* Each page had a free verse or rhyming verse written by people all over the world—actual, regular people who submitted their work to this small publisher specializing in religious poetry. She'd smile and read some to me. "They're so beautiful. Listen to the words." Then she'd touch my hand and read some more. Like me, she had a thing for the texture of how words were grouped and what they felt like. Like me, she drank their juices and grasped the groove of literature. Paired with the watercolor flowers, cottages, and snow-covered hill, she cherished those simple stories very much.

After she died in 2012, my mom made sure I got a handful of those books. The reason my grandma received those mini books every few months from this small publisher was because she donated to various rosary organizations and Catholic charities. When I say donate, I mean ten dollars here, or if it was the holidays, probably a twenty-dollar bill. She had a small and specific budget. One that she paid close attention to and used with her heart.

Genetics *or* character traits within the sensory arena run strong, as my youngest often asks for me to tickle her arm. We'll be in the middle of a couch-snuggle watching her favorite show, and she'll roll up her sleeve and put her arm in the position I can reach and ask, "Mommy, can you tickle my arm?" I have some theories about why we respond so well, and it has to do with something we refer to in Reiki—meridians. How our arms and legs house invisible lines like a roadmap, all leading back to our nerve centers. All capable of pressing us down or keeping us light on our feet.

Currently, I need my husband to gently apply pressure to my hands at night. After a day of typing I like him to find the space between my thumb and index finger and press. Then I ask him to pull each finger gently for a pop. Finally, a gentle twist of my hair in various parts of my scalp.

When I have a major headache, I binge watch Dr. Justin Tubio of Instagram give his neck adjustments to patients—the cradling of the neck. The occipital lift. Look it up. It's like you feel your own pain dissolve after a few watches. Don't judge. We all have our ways to heal.

No matter how old I get, I always go back to my aunt Connie's den couch during those summers at the sidewalk sale—the nights we relaxed and watched TV and set the timer for the arm tickle. That was the origin of exhalation from the day's sensory overload.

Texture of Voices

The bands and genres we listened to as children are both formative and memorable. People hold certain bands, vocalists, and songs dear to their hearts because of what their parents or aunts or grandparents played in the house growing up. It's a beautiful thing. We associate gatherings, people, summers, holidays, neighborhoods, first loves, bad romances, and everything in between when we hear certain music. This is not significant to only me.

Voices sent me through detailed narratives and films in my brain. My wacky brain takes in the sounds and texturizes them in ways that allow me to feel either calm, or hyper. Sad, excited, bored, exhilarated. All of it—sometimes from moment to moment it can shift. The combination of treble and bass launch me on journeys in my brain. The chords tell me stories without words. The sound of some voices were like imaginary yet very real friends.

Dennis DeYoung of Styx has a voice like my favorite macaroni and cheese. When I heard him, I was at ease and so nestled in that I'd think to myself, *How can I ever live without his voice? Can I sustain this level of happiness when "Babe" ends?* As soon as he'd belt those words I'd know life was pretty okay at eight years old. I knew dinner would be soon, and my dad's iceberg lettuce and croutons would sit next to his glass of my mom's homemade iced tea.

I asked my friend Gina this question about voices from her childhood. There are certain friends who understand the question. Her choice was Daryl Hall and John Oates. She's not wrong. Daryl has a "hush little girl" about his voice that can lower your shoulders and make your drive to work more hopeful. Daryl makes you feel like maybe you can eat that third piece of pizza and not feel bad about yourself because you're as perfect as you need to be.

As a kid, the *Private Eyes* album was popular in my house, and "Head Above Water" made me lose my mind. I'd get a giant spark of energy and shake the living room floor. I'd dance so hard and with so much love in my heart for these two men's voices. My two pop-loving uncles urging me to stomp harder and live lighter.

Anita Baker's "Sweet Love" felt like a lullaby from my belly button up to the top of my skull. Anita's voice oozed like braids of silk and the most luscious red rose petals you could grow in New Jersey soil. Impossibly perfect. I wanted to rub the song against my cheek every time I pressed play on the cassette. Her voice was like a favorite aunt to me—her voice telling me that all would be okay in the late 1980s, even though my feet stunk and my hair was a giant frizz bomb. Her voice was telling me that life would go on and time was the answer to friendships that felt sour some days. Time and change. She told me that even if Mike P. Liked Stacey more than me now, someday he'd regret it, and wish he were smarter when I was his girlfriend.

Why would I need these imaginary relatives when my aunts and uncles were already a safe space of solace? Because one can never have too many safe voices that sew up the boo-boos of life. Crushes who don't look your way. Mean girls who tell you're not good enough, or boys who tell you your biceps are too muscular. You know. Important things to a ten- and eleven-year-old.

Julio Iglesias was like my long-lost Spanish uncle who liked to sing in various languages. His voice mended the blues of daily life too, but more importantly, reminded me we were having company over. Which was always exciting in the early 1980s. For those of you who read *Italian Bones in the Snow*, you know that Julio meant it was time for me to clear off the bookshelves and coffee table and get the Windex out for a pre-company cleaning. Turns out he can sing in about fourteen languages, but the ones I remember listening to were Portuguese, Spanish, German, English, and Italian. It didn't matter which he chose. It all sounded like a kind uncle telling me that I was a good kid and that if I loved my family and did my chores and wished well to others, I'd be fine. And maybe, just maybe, if I was nicer to Sara than she was to me (Sara was my very rude friend in the neighborhood), I'd feel better than if I gave her the middle finger back.

o

My favorite and brightest memory of a song sung by Julio Iglesias is "Wo Bist Du." It's sung in German, and it has the best acoustic guitar riff as an intro. I highly recommend adding it to your favorites. When I was young, of course, I imagined him saying, "More beef stew." At this, my mom chuckled, and it sort of stuck. I'll say this about Julio's contribution to my love of language in general: perhaps it explains my penchant for phonemic awareness and why my innate skill to teach reading surpasses the norm. Julio's enunciation and pronunciations were crisp. You hear every syllable. The way he revels and respects every language he sings in, whichever one he is serenading with, he expresses the bend and flow. In turn, the listener develops a sort of respect for it too. If you've never heard Julio Iglesias, welcome to your first track: "Wo Bist Du."

Your second track of Julio's to become acquainted with is "Non Si Vivi Cosi"—an Italian love song that translates to "Can't Live Like This." Now for me, it's not about the lyrics, but rather the memory of my grandmother singing along with him, as if he were swaying right next to her petite frame and giant smile. She loved that song, and then my mom did, and now I do. They were both feeling his love serenade, while I simply feel the 1983 joy that was my life on Mulberry Place in the living room with the hazelnut colored carpet. Or sometimes I'd listen to it at Grandma Yola's kitchen table in her apartment in Nutley. No matter the location, Julio's vocals tore through me like taffy. Can taffy tear through? I just like the way that sounds.

°

My dad's favorite band was Little River Band. Back then I had no idea they were from Australia. I only knew they sounded like men who were my dad's best friends. My dad and all his co-workers from Public Service Energy and Gas. This one requires some in-depth explanation. We lived closest to the Garden State Parkway at 1024 Mulberry Place. So all of my dad's PSE&G co-workers would meet at our house in the wee hours of dawn and leave their cars there. They'd take turns driving to Newark every day, for the hour and fifteen minutes each way. There was something about the vibe of the Little River Band and the timing of when I fell in love that reminds me of the PSE&G guys.

My nutty little brain used to even imagine my dad's co-workers as the band, belting out "Night Owls" since they tended to work the night shift. If you watched *Three's Company* or *WKRP* as a kid, you understand the place my brain was in—the quintessential early 1980s, late 1970s energy of the working-class man. Briefcase and coffee in hand, soon behind the wheel of a Toyota Corolla or a Nissan Sentra, cigarette hanging. The guy with the family to feed, often a former Army reserve guy, with little or no college. I'd hear these songs by Little River Band, and, just like that, I had an entire world in my head. Because their voices had that much texture between the notes. To this day, I really love that band. The basslines are clutch, and the harmonies on fire.

°

When I was in college, my need for certain musical textures was at a peak because as we age, our needs and habits change—just like our overall lifestyle. In those early adult years, I found myself straying from the comfy uncles and positioning myself in life with the voices like Gavin Rossdale, Tori Amos, Ani DiFranco, Bjork, and Eddie Vedder. Now, of course, it's about popular culture in many ways, but I swear it was also the same thing I experienced when I was a child. It transcended entertainment and mood. It was to mitigate sensory urges, ignite urges, quell pain, ignite pain. I could feel their voices in a deep place in my chest and the song would resonate throughout my body and help me heal or bust—either way.

Even now when I hear Everlast's vocals in "What It's Like," there is a place in the depths of my youthful femme core that lusts after him, or rather, his voice. I think we hear their pains, bliss, fears, and celebrations in their vocals, whether they are singing or speaking. When I listened to Dave Grohl tell his life story, I heard love for life in his voice. I heard the appreciation that he feels for music and his mom. Sometimes you can hear a sense of humor, self-awareness, and shame in people's sounds too. Or maybe just sensory people can hear it?

Again, a centuries old concept that music has healing powers, but I've never stopped wondering whether the vocals also contain true love for the sensory-seekers and fingernail gnawers. I wonder if much of our regulation lives in the chords and vocals of the songs we enjoy most, or the songs that settle us back into the colonies of our memories. I wonder whether a song acts like a plush armchair, therapy dough, or anything else that can keep the nerve frenzies calm.

Billy's Tongue

A perfect storm happened in 1990 for the sensory-me. I was beginning to understand what being horny meant. There's no need for me to be elegant about the language here because there's nothing elegant about middle school horniness. I was twelve and there was this music video by Billy Idol called "Cradle of Love." We all knew it, we all waited for it, and we all watched MTV or VH-1with our mouths slightly parted. Now, up until this point here's what I knew: I had an opening down below, it was sensitive, and something was supposed to rub over, across, and near it. At twelve, that's all I knew, or admitted, to know about my pink nerves.

It should be noted that this was two years before my mom started to pay attention to MTV on the family room TV, deciding "No more!" *Too late mom.* I saw what I needed to see already. I saw the asses and the boobs of a few "dancers" and the mouth of Steven Tyler wide open ready to lick all of those things. Guns and Roses will not trash my mind now that I am suddenly a freshman in high school. *Billy Idol however, alerted me to my own sexuality two years ago, Mom.* Of course, I never told her any of that. Let's back up to the dark apartment on some unnamed city block.

So there's this young neighbor girl around sixteen years old who knocks on the apartment door of an older man. Likely, he's about thirty years old, and because there was no dialogue about anything related to the inappropriateness of the age gap and her being a minor, it was what it was: 1990. PS—I'd never let my kids watch this portrayal of the fantasy of a minor. But again, I didn't see or understand that aspect as a middle-schooler in 1990. I only saw the lust and desire that this man had for this girl. And well, I wanted to be her in many ways. Or so I thought. I didn't *really*. I wanted fantasy. I wanted the tingle.

What I did learn from this video was my own potential and power as a female. I learned how the female body can spark certain feelings in onlookers. Basically, this video taught me what it meant to turn someone on—something I wouldn't practice until years after, but the awareness was there. Isn't that the first step toward truth?

Once this unnamed neighbor girl enters the business professional's apartment, she claims her stereo is broken and asks if she can play her cassette in his stereo. Oh, the days of directed dialogue, leading up to the music video's plot before the music even begins! His apartment is posh, modern, and clearly urban in the white privilege sense of the word. She pops the cassette in, and Billy Idol graces the large canvas on the man's apartment wall, further illustrating this man's status in the world as an art collector. As Billy lip syncs his own song, the girl begins to strip down to her bra and skirt and performs some basic seductive dance moves. Acting aloof and as if she's in her own world, but clearly knowing exactly what she's doing as the man trembles, drops his glass, and fidgets all over his apartment. He's in such a startled state, uncertain of where his eyes should be, and really where he should be in terms of the entire apartment. I mean, he should've asked her kindly to leave, but Billy

Idol and the girl's black lingerie have him in a chokehold. Same as my eyes.

It all made my crotch tingly. The movement of her body and the man's awareness of her made me think about my own femininity and what I was able to conjure if given the opportunity. I didn't have breasts yet because I was a late bloomer, but I knew they'd be dazzling enough to get a second glance from boys in a couple years' time. At that point, I had never kissed a boy with tongue—only pecks on the cheek. Now, I am a believer in art and its influence, but I *do not,* under any circumstance believe that art can force people to do things they're not supposed to do. Art cannot cause a person to harm someone else or in this case, find an older man and seduce him with a Billy Idol-led strip tease. We have free will, and when we are guided through life with rights and wrongs from role models; we make our own decisions.

Because though my crotch tingled and I enjoyed this video, I didn't have sex until I was almost nineteen years old. Orgasms? Many, but never from actual sex. The discernment is stupid, but I'm saying it anyway.

The other music videos that created a bit of a nerve-ending ruckus in my pants were "Rag Doll" by Aerosmith and "Cold Hearted" by Paula Abdul. "Rag Doll" was about Steven Tyler's sexy-ugly face more than anything else. His mouth made me feel things. The way he led with it, a kid with raging hormones couldn't help but envision the way he'd use those lips on my mouth. The last minute and a half of the video was what got me. Steven kissing the woman on the porch. The opening scene of the video was the drummer banging between a bass and a snare drum being held upright in the street. For a sensory-me, the drumbeat set the thrilling, sex-in-the-air pace. The drumbeat got me in a headspace of what I didn't even know about yet—a sort of Burlesque peep show, Amsterdam energy where people strut, tongues hung out, and people moaned behind closed doors.

Paula Abdul's "Cold Hearted" is the most obvious in its sensuality—a bunch of scarcely clothed dancers slipping and sliding all over each other's bodies and with facial expressions that invoked nothing but sex on display. That video was a music-centric orgy with really cool outfits and dance moves—the way the human bodies sort of slither over and around each other, like it was what they were born to do. I mean, isn't it? The thing about these videos and their appearance on my TV was that you never really knew *when* they'd be on. Maybe I was in tune to the latest best video countdown, and it was highly likely they'd be in the rotation? Or maybe, it was just a stroke of luck.

Yes, I said stroke.

I'd watch from the corner of my eye. My wide eye. My parents never really noticed. The things that really counted were invisible anyway, like the tingling in the body and the rush of something warm filling in the spaces, and the acute awareness of my femininity.

It makes me chuckle that the "Paradise City" video was the catalyst for my mom to say, "No more MTV for a while! It's garbage." Oh Mom ... if you only knew. Axl Rose had nothing on Steven and Billy. Maybe to other kids, but there was something about the entire direction of the "Rock the Cradle" video. The way it was shot, the darker lighting, and the many red paint colors in the apartment scenario. Or Billy's tongue.

Was it the worst thing in the world to learn of the crotch tingle from Music Television? Rock and roll has been synonymous with sex since the beginning of time, so why should it stop at pop music? The instances in which most of us learn about the crotch tingle range from posters, commercials, sitcoms, movies, magazine pages all the way to the real-life waiters or waitresses taking our order at the local pizzeria when we're thirteen years old. Art can be sex, and I think that's fabulous.

at prop [illegible] For instance, [illegible] in which most [illegible] learn about the [illegible] movies, may [illegible] the [illegible] w[illegible] [illegible]

Marley's

When I was fourteen years old my dad brought me to the local ice cream hut on Route 37 in Toms River called Marley's Ice Cream—family owned since 1955 and known for their incomparable flavor. Originally a Carvel, the owner transformed the business into his own. I filled out the intimidating application, then about a week later, received the phone call that I'd begin my training in two weeks. When I tell you that these positions at Marley's Ice Cream were coveted ones, I do not exaggerate.

This family-owned ice cream joint had a long waitlist for teens wanting a job, so I didn't know why we were bothering. My family didn't have a "name" in the town, nor did my parents care about that kind of thing. I guess my dad figured I needed money to pay for my music-buying habit and eventually my car, so might as well apply everywhere. Well. I got in. I didn't quite grasp the reality of how intense the job would be.

How do I best outline this training process in one swift comparison? Everything from how you walk, where your hands are, to the way your hair is plastered to your head, to the direction the Styrofoam cups face was critical. There was no scooping because it was soft ice cream (we don't say custard in my town). Every step you take is scripted, every word, every strip of ice cream to the quarter inch, and the way you hang up the phone, all matters. An assembly line of tasks, YOU are the machine, the mechanism, the human with a smile, and not a crumb to be seen from the outside, as you swim in a fishbowl of a building, windows all around. Wait your turn, clean up after yourself, soak the sponges in special sanitizer, stink like bleach for days, and goddess help you if your boss catches you in the backroom with those chopped up peanut butter cups jam-packed in your apron—your mouth ripe with fuzz from the lint balls that made it in with the peanut butter cups and down your teenage throat with an ecstasy only peanut butter and chocolate can initiate.

It's a navy ship. An operating room. A battlefield. A spelling bee. A symphony.

And most of all, a Jersey Shore gift to the masses with a gold star reputation ruined by a single "Is that to go?" *Fuck no.* It's "Is that for here or to go home in a bag?" *There's a difference, Elaina.* And then when you pass this information along in your own time to your friends and family and they say, "Oh my GOD, it's just ice cream." Which is exactly what you're thinking as it's happening and you're getting ripped a new asshole for using the wrong cup for a fruit salad sundae. Yet suddenly you're offended by the comment from others. Now you get it. "It is more than ice cream." Suddenly, you feel pride about your time and training at Marley's because it was sort of a privilege. It was an empire built on consistency and clean lines. And so much patriarchal bullshit in the earlier days.

For every station there were three to four designated sponges, and you could not mix and match, as some required a swipe of the stainless-steel counters and the others the rim of the Styrofoam cups. If any sponge didn't sparkle in its original lemon yellow vibrance, once the spurt of customers ended, hell was raised by the owner's son—a guy you wouldn't want your daughter dating, ever. If the dispensers didn't shine, you were *toast.* If you didn't use the extra five minutes between customer rushes to clean the grooves of the freezers' tracks, well ... you'd never be respected.

"Girls. Wanna chew some tobacco?" Is how it was posed to me and two other sixteen-year-old friends I'd known since elementary school who also worked the night shifts. It was probably late May or early June when the crowds were swelling in anticipation of another booming and bright summer on the Jersey Shore.

"Squeeze it into a ball, then trap it inside your cheek, nice and tight. And suck." Suck we did. Falter and stumble we did. High as kites. We didn't think twice about trying it, probably to impress the boys' club. My sensory stuff got a long dinner break when that chewing tobacco kicked into gear. As harsh and offensive as the boys were, they were also the ones we had to stand up to and give them something to be shocked about. We had to show them that we weren't boring. Two of my friends chose more involved measures with two of the men. I did the chewing tobacco like a champ but dated guys my own age outside of work.

I remember a very specific Sunday afternoon when I was on the schedule for the noon-to-five shift. I pulled my cheddar-yellow Marley's short sleeve polo over my head, ate my usual ham and cheese on rye with potato chips and a pickle for lunch, and pinned my hair up into its hairspray cement state. My mom was simmering the foundations of her Sunday tomato sauce in the kitchen while I ate. My dad was tinkering in the garage until it was time for me to go to work. I was about sixteen and only had a driver's permit, so my parents still drove me places.

I arrived at 11:55 sharp, as anything after that is considered late, and it would be remembered, lectured over, and mentally marked in either Ruth or Randy's head. I followed the usual procedure of washing my hands in front of Ruth. Tying up my apron. Doublechecking that not a single hair on my head did anything but stay plastered with its herd.

And then Ruth approached me. She stood a solid yard from me, and one foot at a time, met me up close. "Hmm. I smell something." She sniffed the shoulder of my shirt. "Onions." Her glare could've sliced through granite. "Elaina. You can't smell like this. Go home and change. Call your mom." She paced back and forth between the sink area and the back stockroom.

"But the customers are on the outside of the store. They won't smell it. My mom was making sauce today." Out of anyone, I should have understood how my oniony smell could easily offended customers once I opened the front window and they got a whiff.

"Elaina. Call your mom. You can't smell like that here."

"Really?" I was so embarrassed, and she was so acerbic.

"You smell like onions. Which then smells like B.O., even though I know it's onions. *Elaina.* You can't smell like that at work."

"Ok."

"It's in the details, Elaina," Ruth said.

Over the next six years of working for Marley, the owner, and Ruth, his daughter, I learned this was true to the highest extent. The details. You say "Is that for here or to take home in a bag?" Not "to go." See, the difference in elegance? I'm a language person, so it clicked for me. The difference teetered between a phrase you hear at a fast-food drive thru versus one at an establishment with a sparkling local reputation.

Working at Marley's Ice Cream was very much an extended game of memory too. Not only did we have to know the correct container for the many menu choices, but we were also not allowed to use a pen and paper to take customer orders, unless it was a phone order. Even if they ordered fifteen items. No pen.

o

After working for Marley himself for three years solid, it was time to ask for a raise. Instead of $5 an hour, I sought $5.25. He said "no." No to the girls. Yes to the boys. My first experience with inequality in the workplace. Our Queen Ruth fought for us. She was technically very much our boss too, so she had every right to pound hard until her dad said yes. He never did, so I left. I left to work for a local farmer's market who paid me fifty cents more an hour. Less cleanliness, more space to breathe, and no night shifts. Ruth was livid at her father for letting me walk out over a quarter.

Ruth fixed that by opening her own store. Girls only. Ruth schooled us over and over about how men will get away with anything they can. Let me be clear. Toward me and the rest of the girls on staff, these guys who worked at the original store were perfectly nice. They didn't harass us, nor were they overly inappropriate or sexist to our faces. I enjoyed many evenings working and competing with them for quick, neat orders or making them laugh, as they'd do too. Many evenings we'd all find ourselves in the back room, stuffing our waist aprons with Reese's Cups.

Some of the girls I worked with developed hard-core crushes on the guys, and others just flirted incessantly. Some went all the way. I did none of it. I preferred remaining one of the *guys.* Maybe I did flirt minimally, but I had a very serious high school relationship, so I was a happy spectator of the sport.

Marley's Ice Cream gave me sugar, a work ethic, and survival skills.

Puppy Love

Writers have been writing about their first love for years. Readers have been reading about the same. The butterflies in the belly, the needles in the pelvic area, the shivers and sweat on the neck are the usual aspects covered. I'm more interested in the smell combos and the tastes of first loves. The scent memory from behind their ears. The taste of their saliva. Their breath at dusk. Their navel fuzz.

In my town, sports was competitive in high school for as long as I've been a resident in my town. Sports first. Then the arts. See: Toms River Little League 1998, but it began long before that major regional achievement. My high school band camp began in August of 1991, so before any of the other freshman got to set foot inside the school to spy our classrooms or lockers, to find their people, the band kids did. Will I call us band geeks? Perhaps, but there's something about living down the shore. We had too much salt in us to be wholesomely geeky. There was a stripe of surfer in us all, granules of beach somewhere on our bodies from April through October. In my opinion, that kept us from fitting inside the band-geek box completely. Most of us who played instruments were also athletes. That combo made us less likely to be bullied too. But also, more of something else? Trouble-seekers? You decide.

As a freshman, I was ready for it all solely because of Maegen Alt, the oldest daughter of my parents' oldest friends, Bob and Noreen Alt. Maegen drove me around in her clunky blue sedan all summer long with senior friends from marching band. We'd ride around and watch the fireworks in July, go to a few house parties, and maybe some random pick-ups of people who I'd get to know better when the school year opened in six weeks. In Maegen's car was where I first heard Tori Amos, then Mental Jewelry by Live. In the backseat of Maegen's car was where I learned she was popular for the good reasons—she loved and accepted everyone of all shades, spots, and personalities. In the backseat of Maegen's car was where I learned that being in marching band was not so geeky after all. It was sort of the place to be in our school climate. Again, because I'd venture to say that eighty percent of the band members were also athletes. I was very lucky to have Maegen and be under her wing before school even began. She really paved the pathway for me into a new school and made my high school entrance less overwhelming.

My tribe of band geeks found me, mid-August, with our field show preparations in hand.

Mr. M, the band director and the assistant band director, a very quiet guy named Mr. G, distributed our instrumental parts; we learned them, memorized them, and then transitioned the counting of our feet in formations on the grass outside the band room. Cars driving by witnessed our clumsy feet and chaotic pace— always the truth until everyone nailed their parts. The practice field faced Old Freehold Road. I'd say a few days into things, I noticed Gregg. I also noticed Keith. Gregg was a freshman like me, and Keith was a senior. Gregg had braces, floppy, feathery dirty blond hair, and Keith had yellow-blond hair, blue eyes, and was super skinny. Gregg had thighs of soccer-player steel. Like the kind you want to bite. I'm a biter. Keith was very into me—me, the little freshman brass player with no fear, coming to band practice all sweaty and toned from field hockey practice.

And though Keith was very funny and kind, I had my eye on Gregg, who could barely look my way, as he was bashful to the highest heights. He was tall, tan, always in soccer cleats, and his shy dimpled smile drove me crazy. Which made me want him to look my way even more. Trina, the tall, thin, brunette bells player had her eye on Gregg too. She was delightfully feminine and had legs for miles. I had semi-long legs with muscle tone that could crack walnuts. She was femme, and I was rough around the edges. My advantage over Trina was my overconfidence in almost everything I put my hands on. It's served me well and horribly my whole life. Don't be impressed at all.

We all socialized from day one, across the grade levels, which is another kind of cool thing about band. Band experiences knew no age. We were in this half-awkward, half-exhilarating time together. We laughed in between routines at Paul R's jokes and Mike S's sexist rants. We all bonded over the weeks. I flirted with Gregg. He blushed. Trina flirted with Gregg. He blushed. Keith flirted with me. I flirted back. Keith would wait for me in the school parking lot and drive me to lunch at Al's Pizza up the road because we were allowed to do that in 1991. I went to senior parties with Keith. I kind of liked him, but really, I liked Gregg.

Gregg picked *me* over Trina one October afternoon when school had been in session for weeks already. I crushed Keith's heart all over that field show grass. Not on purpose. I mean, nothing happened between me and Keith except for the promise of *maybe*. It was the smells. Skin. Neck. Hair. Oils. Gregg's neck skin chemistry. Like animals in the wild. Or hydrogen with oxygen. Therein lies our humanity. Our primal instincts. I needed Gregg's smell on mine. He wore no cologne. I cannot even describe it because it was science. All I can say is, he wasn't Italian because I am not attracted to the smell of Italian guys. Ever. From the moment my lips tasted his cheek in the hallway of A-Wing, I inhaled my foreseeable future.

We started dating, and he was in for more than he had bargained with me, but he got acclimated fast, and we were totally and absolutely in a creamy kind of entanglement. French kissing by the lockers, in the stairwell, in our family rooms when we made sure our parents were nowhere around. In his basement, in the instrument room when everyone else crowded out. In the back of the band bus. It was a teenage mess of heat and glorious stink.

He became jealous over everything. I couldn't keep my loyalty loyal enough for him. I never cheated; I just flirted a little. You couldn't keep me in a cage tight enough, but I didn't do anything over the line. He would get bent out of shape, write me serious letters about how he and his brother would beat the crap out of each other. I would comfort him. We were together for almost three years. When we became upperclassmen, things started leaning into the ugly, and it was because I wanted to know other people's smells. He was ready to marry me.

I must rewind to the beginning, so you see how Gregg stuck to me, the way my teeth found that headrest in my mom's white Buick at age six. This relationship was built on another planet. A true first love. We ran together, swam together, spent holidays together, got lost in geometry homework together. We played jazz together. Had a field show duet together. Saw LA together. All before the age of sixteen. We did not, however, have sex together. I *might* have, but he was not about to, and for that I should've thanked him. It would have made our breakup ten times more disastrous.

We'd hang out at both our houses, as neither of us drank alcohol in high school. It was a major source of connection for us. I can't pinpoint the reason we didn't drink, but we individually chose that and just happened to find each other to be the same. It wasn't like he influenced me or vice versa. We simply didn't like it. Don't imagine we were prudes. We liked licking each other from head to toe. It just never required or craved the presence of beer or rum or whatever our peers were imbibing on the weekends. And they knew it. Nobody flinched or pushed, I have to say. They just knew Elaina and Gregg didn't drink.

We were not interested in fitting a mold. Gregg and I had a bond that stemmed from an intergalactic place. Like we had known each other from a past life and would continue to run into each other in other non-Earthly places, even when the romantic part ended. Because even when we fought, as teenagers do, there was this deeper clenching of the soul that endured. I know it was there, and I'd never ask him or contact him to ask him the same. I simply knew. It was far-reaching, and it had to do with how the joys and troubles in our hearts were compatible, rather than the people we are today.

Gregg's parents' house smelled like wood. It was one of the only houses I recall in my childhood or adolescence that skipped the carpeting. It all felt very Vermont-like and English-countryside or something in that kind of ballpark. They also had this back room adjacent to their kitchen, which kind of felt like an addition and maybe was their library? It's where they put their Christmas tree and a giant clear view of the backyard, since the windows were floor to ceiling. It was the room where his mom practiced her cello. They were a family of skilled musicians and chamber vocalists. When I tell you this wasn't a typical first love experience, I mean it. His family all fell in love with the salty Italian girl who had way too much self-confidence than she should have, and my family fell in love with his high IQ and good-boy disposition. His parents sang in Baroque choirs. Mine went to Caesars in Atlantic City. I never told my parents how dark it got towards the end of our relationship.

He had clear braces. It never bothered me when we were kissing, even if I did get a piece of onion from his Jersey Mike's turkey and cheese now and again. A lot of our time was spent on a long yellow band bus with Sami, Alison, Tim, and Matt S to and from north Jersey towns competing in field shows or playing football games. Some weekends it was Friday and Saturday. Other weekends one of the two. Either way, the smell of oil and vinegar subs (you may know them as hoagies or footlongs) still hits my nose at the memory-artery so potently.

In between unwashed band uniforms across bus seats, left-over napkins and sub wrappers peppered the scene. It was a disaster and it stunk to the high heavens. No one ever sat properly on the rides up. Gregg and I would often just nestle in far back on the bus and have our own cave of cuddles and games. When we were in moods or if something happened during the day, we'd detach and ignore each other. One time we fought because I spent too much time being interested in Mike Reuter's sneakers. Another time we fought because I was totally obsessed with the same song Jim Snell loved by some random '90s alternative band.

Gregg was slightly possessive, but I always forgave it because I could be a space cadette at times and get enraptured by the smallest curiosities surrounding people. And though it came off as flirting, it wasn't. I did like the attention from the other boys, but I was *all* his. I really liked digging into people's weird preferences and likes. We were surrounded by musicians, flag twirlers, and color guard devotees. So much glorious weirdness to dig into.

The smell that kicks in these high school years with Gregg was the smell of valve oil used on our baritone horns when the keys got sticky. Which honestly, I haven't laid my nostrils on in decades since my teenager plays the viola. It was an untidy business to oil the valves on brass instruments. It sinks into your skin for days.

Looking back, I doubt I would've endured four full years of stage band, jazz band, marching band, and special state orchestras if I hadn't had Gregg to motivate me. He motivated me to be as good as he was with the actual music. He motivated me to be as fluent in "look at me and how bold I am with my instrument" among the patriarchal leaders whose care we were under those years. I remember women musicians who stood out and earned major parts and roles, but that was more performative and to meet a quota. I could tell by the posturing of the men in authority how uncomfortable it made them at times. The mood that permeated the music arena was still full of machismo, so I was there for the fight.

Phone call between two fourteen-year-olds in 1992:

"What are you doing?" His voice giggly.

"Hold on. Get out of here. I'm on the phone!!!"

Younger brother: "Mom she's been on the phone too long!"

"Stop. I need a few more minutes." I lay on my brown bedroom carpet and put both of my legs up on the wall, as extended and as straight as possible. My tailbone flat, my butt on a climb up against the wall as if it's leading the stretch for me.

"Sorry. My brother."

"It's okay. Where are you?"

"I'm in my room. It's so hot in here. Do you have air conditioning?" My eyes zone in on a missed patch of hair on my kneecap. Damn kneecaps.

"Yes. You don't?"

"No. It's so hot." I sniff my armpit. It is so god damn hot and the carpet doesn't help. Hot mud brown. I smell the pizza downstairs.

"Yeah dude. It's hot out." He's probably as cool as a cucumber in his den next to his Cocker Spaniel.

"Band was weird. Tim is nuts." I push my legs even hard against the wall. I like my legs. Especially when they are fully extended.

"I know. We went to elementary school together. He's a riot." His dimples are probably popped out now.

"I like Sami a lot. She's pretty right?" I bite a stray cuticle from my thumbnail. I get a tiny flake of nail polish in my mouth along with it.

"Not as pretty as you."

"Really?"

"Yep."

"But my hair is freakin' frizzy." I bend my left leg and make a sort of formation of a lower-case B with my legs, still pressed into my peach wall.

"Your hair is thick and Italian."

"I guess. Can you hold on a second? Ma! Save me a pepperoni slice."

Mom: "Your brother needs the phone!"

"Five minutes!!! Ok. sorry. I have dance tomorrow night. My favorite night of the week." Oh my god, stretching is heaven. But it's so HOT in here.

"Cool. Yeah. That's cool."

"What are you having for dinner?"

"I don't know."

"Oh. Do you like Mrs. Thornborough?"

"She's nice. She's a really great runner."

"I know. I see her out on the track." I should run more.

"I NEED THE PHONE."

"Two minutes."

"Ma!!!!!!!!"

"I have to go. See you in the morning?"

"Yes. Be good. Good night."

"Night."

Chills. Sweat. I love him. I hang up the phone, put my legs behind my head and roll backwards to standing.

o

We could never get enough of each other, and we argued a lot, but we made up a lot too. We broke up before we hit the three-year mark, right around spring of Junior year. It left a full year in high school for us to try on other people, but it wasn't without so much drama and jealousy. All very normal teenage bullshit, yet in the end, we took each other to Senior Prom. We rode down an hour to Wildwood, New Jersey together to meet the drinking, hotel-hanging, boardwalk-slinging crowd, with no intentions of hooking up. We did find great comfort still, in being next to each other as non-drinkers. Also, we both had to wake up super early to head back for the Founders Day Parade the next day. It was a major rule for senior band members, so up we were, and sped he did, back up the Garden State Parkway in this strange June-morning-hazy silence that haunts me still if I think it over. We blasted the Beastie Boys, and without saying much to each other, we said a lot. Our year and time close by was ending. Even though we had been broken up over a year at that point, you could cut our history and connection with a knife. The wires were straggly, severed, and the lightbulbs iffy, but we weren't a dead fuse by any means. First loves can be ... complicated.

About a year after we finally called it quits, we dated other people, yet somewhere in between it all, I wanted him back. I asked him to lie on our living room carpet next to the giant speakers while I played "Till the End of Time" by Mariah Carey because it was the only way I could express it. He did without flinching. I have no recollection of what he said after. But he definitely loved me the same way for a long time. We both just ... kept on living and never went back there.

I interrupt this memoir to address the behavior of teachers of days gone by ...

After reflecting on the first puppy love of my life where marching band was our main setting, every day, and many hours on weekends, trips across the country, etc. I thought I'd slip this chapter in as a chance to speak up—originally these next few paragraphs illustrated a single high school teacher scandal that I witnessed up close. While editing this book in the summer of 2024, I learned that exposing specific individuals would be hurtful to their family members (not mine)—individuals who are so kind and lovely, and therefore I didn't have the heart to keep the scandal on the pages. I should note that this individual told me *not* to compromise my art. You never know who is related to whom, especially when they are nothing like their parent. I am happy with my decision to write the following material instead.

I was sixteen when I experienced the bulky weight of being a pretty girl with brains and talent. Instead of making this chapter about me, I decided to give life to the topic of teacher-bullies in general and learn that many other women (and men) experienced similar encounters and unfortunate events related to toxic masculinity (and inappropriate sexualization by women) before it had a place in our societal dialogue.

The following are written in second and third person. Because often, difficult subjects require second person.

The Men in Charge of Her Art

Picture it: 1992-95, a suburban high school in central New Jersey. There is a clear line drawn between the boys and the girls who play instruments—and the men in charge recognize the talent of both, yet the girls are treated with much less praise and respect *because* they are girls. There are exceptions. The exceptions are the smiles and giggles. If you don't do that for the men, you stay second chair. You take longer to advance, despite your hard work and natural talent. You have hurt the fragile ego of the men, and so for daily lessons and countless concerts, field shows, trips, you hang out in the back. You stay quiet. Because you refuse to smile for him. You know what's going on. You don't have a voice though. Because you're kind of a bitch in his eyes.

But She Doesn't Look Like a Scholar?

Picture it: 2011, a suburban high school in central New Jersey. A girl experiments with her hair color. The same girl is ambitious, diligent, and works hard in her academic classes. The teacher doesn't see her or hear her and goes as far as to tear apart her notebook and throw it out the second-floor window of a classroom in front of the entire class. Likely because her hair is bright red from a bottle. A creative artist who likes fashion. She's a loser in his eyes because deep down he is the loser.

Keep Your Sex Life Out of It

Picture it: 1971, a north New Jersey suburban high school. A boy has an English teacher who throws her cleavage around like it's candy—she wants him and everyone to hone in on her breasts while she discusses the sexual nuances of life instead of discussing the novel they read. She leans in close, asks the students about their sex lives. She is not supposed to be a teacher, but she is. For many years. Nobody says anything to authority because they're terrified they'll be called liars.

Words That Stick to the Ribs

Picture it: 1997, a central New Jersey suburban high school. A girl trying to pass chemistry. She is a writer and a reader, and so science requires more effort. She has a job, friends, and a lot of goals. The guy teacher hands back their recent test—one that she studied extra hard for since the other ones perplexed her, no matter how hard she studied. Maybe his study guides lacked substance. Teacher tosses the test on her desk:

"See Mr. E (talking to a colleague). All you have to do to get a kid to work harder is to fail them a few times."

Same teacher looks the girl in the eyes and says, "You will never amount to anything."

Let this one sit with you a minute. The way it sat with her for years. Shame sticks to the ribs.

She's Too Young for You

Picture it: 1999, a suburban central New Jersey high school. The male teacher cannot stop staring. Into her eyes, up and down her body. Stays close by whenever he can. He even tells her how beautiful she is, but it's not her fault, nor is it her job to stop doing anything. She's not flirting back. She's being her friendly, sixteen-year-old self, concerned with succeeding in school—getting straight As and being a well-rounded, college-bound person. He doesn't get it. It continues for years after because a student remains in high school for four years. It's his job to stop. It's not her job to be less friendly and less enthusiastic about being the best student.

Let Me Lie for You

Picture it: 2019, a suburban central New Jersey fifth-grade classroom. The boy is devoted to his cello but loves the holiday festivities in class. He is a tad bummed about having to leave for a half hour of cello lessons during the holiday party in class, but knows it's the right thing to do until the middle-aged classroom male teacher pulls him aside and says, "Want me to lie to the music teacher and say you're absent today so you can stay for the party?"

And when mom calls the teacher out over the phone for modeling this deceitful behavior to her child, he reacts by bashing the music teacher and cursing her out.

Most teachers would be reprimanded, but he is the principal's friend, and he "knows" people. No one holds him accountable for much. He even likes to squirt kids with their own water bottles. Because he is "cool."

Follow Me

Picture it: 1960, a small Catholic school in southern New Jersey, grade eight. The middle-aged layperson teacher (male) needs supplies from the closet known as the cloak closet. He repeatedly chooses wide-eyed pretty girls to enter the closet with him. The rest of the class notices. They wonder. He only calls on the happy, peppy ones. The ones less likely to tell someone all about the cloak closet.

Present Day

My days as a full-time, or even part-time classroom and special education teacher in public schools are gone, but I do spend many days a week as a substitute teacher in a performing arts high school in central New Jersey.

I see support. I see kindness. I see respect and appropriate behaviors. I see advocacy.

There is hope. There are many good people out there. There are still extraordinary teachers in the world.

Girl Problems

I was a spectator of my brother's sports up until about fifth grade when I didn't have to tag along because I had more friends or could hang out at home by myself. Jazz class kept me happy once a week at The Dance Centre, leading up to my big June recital every year since kindergarten. Despite loving dance class, I begged to play soccer like my brother, but my dad always said no. I wanted to sweat, push through competition pain, and run back and forth on a field with a purpose. I loved the aftermath and orange slices that followed a victory. Dad maintained ... *no*.

The no was not because my dad didn't believe in my abilities. The truth—it wasn't in our budget for me to do more than dance class and my brother to play a sport every season. That being said, my dad involved me in the soccer Saturdays by giving me the clipboard with the team member names. I was attendance-checking sister. Organization—dad's love language. He had everyone's name listed in his own all-caps handwriting. I'd place a check mark next to every boy's name as they arrived on the field in their orange-and-white Toms River Hawks uniforms. The scene was neat for a Libra like my dad: boy on the field, girl as secretary. Everything balanced on a Saturday morning after eggs and toast.

One foggy soccer Saturday, instead of hanging out to watch the boys play—the names I had put a neat check next to upon arrival—I decided to venture off to the playground on the outskirts of the soccer fields. For the life of me, I cannot remember who was with me. *A family friend? A sister of one of the other players?* Someone was. Because that someone had to retrieve my mom from the sidelines of the game while I sat and inhaled the fear. The Mother Mary totally protected me in the moment after the fall. I know it. If *she* didn't then the femme-fog-gods of fourth-graders-lingering-in-the-wet-dew-of-April did. Protectors of pain. Guardians of vaginas.

I veered off closer to the bony woods. The air hung thick with April's vinegar tears, ushering me and someone I've apparently blocked from my ten-year-old moment in time, toward the playground. In 1987 this playground was comprised of a few rusty chain-link swings, a dented metal slide, some of the coil-spring ponies for the little ones, and a dome-shaped jungle gym. The dome composition was dominated by dozens of hexagonal shapes and very thin bars of blue, yellow, and red. The air spoke in misty breaths. It wasn't a sunny Saturday—like I said—pickled air and fresh New Jersey soil. We played on the swings, stumbled around lazily, and then I decided I'd climb to the top of the thinly-barred jungle gym.

I reached the top easily, as I was, and still am, a highly coordinated human being with good muscle tone. There is such freedom in natural athletic ability, and so if I couldn't score goals or feel the sweat on my neck with the boys on the field, I'd find it myself in this climb. I hung out up top for a while. Until I felt, *maybe I should be a supportive sister and watch the game.*

As my descent began, one of my feet slipped on the dewy bars, damp with spring. It's these kinds of moments right here when your entire female existence is in the hands of the way you're designed. Though, a boy's parts would hurt heavily, there's no splitting of tissue. No destruction of connection.

I landed with my legs spread open, in a straddle. These bars were pure 1980s-playground-metal and about three inches wide. Something didn't feel right, yet I didn't scream, nor wince in pain. It was a moment of *Oh. This isn't good.* My skin lit up in heat and cold at the same time, my brain, dizzy. I found my way down, not by climbing, but through a gentle fall underneath the dome in the open air. I crawled in the dirt under the bottom hexagons and found the nearest bench. I remember imagining I was a forest creature—a slow lumber with caution. I remember thinking, *Oh. I'm not going to have a good few days ahead.* Our brain knows things only when our body knows things. My ten-year-old heart shrunk, my spirit demolished. Being a girl sucked right now. Being a girl split in half.

The person I was with knew something was wrong. *I* knew something was wrong.

I sat there with my plum cotton sweatsuit on, hands on my knees, and stared at the wet ground. The random grass patches. Not a yellow dandelion in sight yet. I knew I slipped. I knew in between my legs was fragile, but I couldn't feel a searing cut or puncture like you do when you fall off your bike and into the gravel with bare knees, or when you step on something in the street like a bottlecap or a cracked rock. This was more of an emotional haunt. I was sweaty and cold. I felt sort of like I had motion sickness, except it was a fuller, duller ache where my pulse both slowed and quickened in no sensible pattern. I longed to be one of the players on the field more than ever now. Running and slicing my cleats across the grass in high hopes. Spinning toward my teammates with victory on my mind.

"Go get my mom," I whispered through my teeth to the mystery person. "Please. Get my mom," I repeated.

My friend brought my mom to me, and I told her what happened. "I think I'm hurt." I pointed to my pelvic area. My mom asked minimal questions and drove me home. I don't remember the car ride. Though, the next part is very clear in my memory. I landed solo in our house's very brightly lit second-floor bathroom. My mom gave me space. The only full bathroom in the house—blue tiles and a lot of clean, sparkly white porcelain, I pulled my pants down. Dried blood and fresh blood in every direction. I peed and it burned. I was badly cut and bruised. I also believe I was in shock because I didn't yell. I didn't panic. Automatic pilot. I wiped what I could manage, then dragged my mom away from our company downstairs. I don't remember who was visiting, but they had also been at the soccer fields watching the game. My mom urged me to lie down on my back on her soft bedspread after she laid out a bathroom towel. She remained calm. Calm but concerned. My thighs were bruised. I was pretty torn up in the vaginal area. My mom had to gently peel my panties off, my thighs smeared in a mess of dried blood.

The worst part of this healing experience in the week to follow was visiting my very kind, but very *man* pediatrician, Dr. Velaswamy. He'd been my doctor since we'd moved from Little Falls to Toms River, so he was all I knew. He was so gentle and so caring, but he was still a man, and I was ten. I had a very traumatic pelvic exam, despite how compassionately he and the staff spoke and moved.

"The material in the vaginal area is the same as the tongue. No stitching needed. She will heal on her own with rest," he said. I remember these words. I smelled so much alcohol and disinfectant. The office always smelled that way, even the waiting room, but that day it was at a maximum level of clinical. That day it was like a habitat, and I felt like an animal. I was given all kinds of creams, huge maxi pads, and sent home.

I stayed home from school for a week. With each day, the blood got less and less on my huge pads. With each day, I was less sore, and more hopeful. My classmates thought I hurt my back badly because that's what I told one of my closest friends. I enjoyed day after day of ham and cheese sandwiches while my mom returned to work. I inhaled ice cream, and *I Love Lucy* reruns. *Mr. Belvedere* and *Perfect Strangers* were in the mix too. It wasn't terrible. I believe it was my very first experience in self-care and spiritual leveling-up. My secret, my shows, my snacks, and my healing, emotionally and physically.

I did heal, but my ten-year-old brain worried about whether I'd be able to have children or if anything would look strange after I healed. Neither of those things happened. It just … healed. The human body, like human emotions, is complex and outrageously miraculous like that. There was a long stretch of time where I totally forgot about this accident. It wasn't until maybe five years ago that I remembered. Those thin-barred dome-shaped jungle gyms only exist anymore in memory or old *Sesame Street* footage. And for good reason. I imagine it all should've set my body on fire in the moment of the fall, yet some cosmic force wouldn't allow it. I am forever grateful for the planets, stars, or feminine guardians that tossed the cloud of numbness my way. It let me melt rather than explode.

Green Tree

Traveling around with my dad in the early 1980s in his 1982 burnt orange Nissan Sentra conjures up the smell of his green tree air freshener hanging by a string from the rearview. Holy smokes did it turn my stomach. I didn't say anything. If I *had* said the words, "Dad. That smell is making me feel sick to my stomach, and it's giving me a headache," his 1980s-dad reply would have been, "It's fine. You'll be fine." And it wasn't that my dad was mean, so don't feel bad for younger me. It was how it was in the 1980s. The cause and effect was completely logical, but my request as the child in the situation was not enough to warrant changing his car smell. I simply dealt with the smell, and eventually I was able to plow through the nausea.

My dad and I have always had an easy language. It's called minimal, and that's how we like it. It's peaceful, fight-free, neither of us in the mood to conjure up any unessential conflict. We like to enjoy the sights, sounds, and smells if there are any worth picking up—soft pretzels, confectionary sugar, things like that if we're in the places where those smells might be accessible.

"Dad, would you mind taking that off? I think it's triggering my sinuses and making me feel nauseated." I was around eight years old with zero rights, zero autonomy in this context. Mouth shut. Parents in charge. Stomach roiling.

The smell was and still is so ... manufactured-plastic smelling. I recently bought one to remember, and then immediately chucked it into the trash. Still overpowering in all the wrong ways. I remember driving around town, and sometimes the state, with him to hardware stores. Sometimes we'd drive an hour just to look at someone's used car that he'd consider buying. I loved that because it was my dad's version of adventure and exploration. I'd watch him open the door of the car that sat on a lawn. Usually there was a sign on the dashboard or taped to the inside windows indicating its price and mileage. He'd tinker with the radio if there was a key for the ignition present—often with the owner right there, watching him with arms folded, hoping he'd make an offer. Then he'd tinker with the windows, the windshield, and together they'd open the hood. My dad knew what he was looking for and at, and I marveled at his knowledge of the machinery.

Later when it was time to find my first car, we'd do the same thing, and I'd end up landing on a 1984 Red Dodge Aries for $500. I paid for it with my money from working at Marley's. The Aries treated me so well for about three years. Despite its inside roof that required thumbtacks to be held up, it was perfect. I still love seeing cars on the side of the road or on lawns for sale. I know they hold adventure and love for the right person. Don't ever scoff at them. If they were cared for properly, they still have life in them. During our previous random New Jersey road trips to investigate used cars, he never bought one. I think he was just curious and hoping, "If the right one strikes me, I will make an offer."

On the way home from our faux car shopping, we'd often stop by Eagle Hardware where better smells careened and crushed all over my earthling face. My condition improved as soon as we entered the doors of Eagle. The sweet smell of cedar wood and sawdust quickly erased air freshener grossness. A love expression for me—directly from Dad in the 1980s, holding my hand into the store full of chainsaws, chain links on huge wheels, and power tools we couldn't afford. It's almost like this was his version of the arts—taking me through this museum of construction and home improvement. Walking with me, hand in hand, showing his love by sharing his love of materials and cogs and gadgets. I felt his love this way since he couldn't and still can't say it out loud. My dad can't hug very easily, so instead, he showed me wall paneling, beams, mailboxes, paints, knobs, and chain choices. I didn't mind at all.

It's in Eagle's Hardware that he'd give me a dime or a quarter so I could snag a handful of the Chiclet gum in the machine by the entrance. I'd always hope for the black and green ones, as they were my favs. The red was too cherry-like, and the white one boring. The flavor only lasted ten minutes before I felt like I was chewing rubber, but it was worth the initial explosion of sugary fruit shaped like squares on my tastebuds.

The next thing that often happened was my dad's spontaneous side. We'd begin at the top of Mulberry Place. It was a hill, and so much fun to ride a bike down, but currently we'd be in the car returning from our road trip and Eagle. He'd pull the car over and place me on his lap and I'd "drive" from the top of Mulberry and down to our house. He'd of course have his hands over mine, but it sure felt like I was in control. I enjoyed it so much.

Those dreary not-quite-spring Saturdays or Sundays with my dad and the stinky green tree on the rearview were some of my favorite days.

Family Room

Hela Young was kind of a gospel figure in our house—her ten-minute segment filled our weeknights, like a sermon we never wanted to miss. She was the patron saint of the New Jersey Lottery, live broadcasted from WOR studios. We'd watch local channel nine in total anticipation as she pulled those tiny white balls from the rumbling plastic machines where the balls flew around like popcorn from forceful air blasts. The way she'd use her fingers to show us the number was so thrilling to younger me, and her annunciation—off the charts! I knew the speech. I knew the red nail color. I knew how wishful my dad was that maybe we'd win the Pick Three one night.

It was truly an event in our home to watch Hela at 8 p.m. sharp and follow along with my dad's one or two lottery tickets. Then when her assistant placed the number disks on the wall behind the machines, it became real—the number combo for the evening a little bigger and brighter for everyone to see. I loved the entire texture of the scene. How I wanted to touch it all. To feel the way the winning number discs fit perfectly onto their designated hooks. That was to make certain all viewers, even the ones tuning in late, knew the winning numbers.

Thinking about Hela Young got me thinking more about our family room on Mulberry Place—the way my parents decorated their home. There was a dramatic touch to their taste, and it still lives in my taste. First and foremost, we had the sad Pagliacci clown. It was a two-foot statue of an extremely sad circus clown wearing a yellow blouse and orange pants and the same orange puffs down his shirt where buttons would typically sit. The way the stone was molded, then painted, gave emphasis to the folds and wrinkles in his costume. I didn't understand that it was art. It didn't scare me either. It perplexed me. It made me think about my mom and why she chose this as a display piece. Like what struck her about this clown that made her want it in our family room? I never asked her. Yet, if I had it in our house, my kids would ask me every other day—*why mom, why*? It's the difference between the conversations we've opened over the years—ask questions about things, people, old ideas, the creepy sad clown in the middle of the room. To be honest, I think having that clown distinguished my home from some of my friends' homes. Their parents had the usual Lenox and collectibles trapped behind their dining room hutches. My parents liked a nice touchable display of art. An expression of who they were. I enjoyed it.

On the wall of our family room, over the original couch upholstered by my dad's cousins, was a metal representation of an amusement park, complete with a Ferris wheel. I wish I had a photo of it so I could describe it in more detail. What I do remember is that the metal was darker brown, with hints of gold in various spots. We left north Jersey to live on the Jersey Shore when I was two years old in 1979, and this piece of amusement park art was a sort of ode to that, if you ask me. My parents loved the beach, the arcades, the sausage sandwiches on the seaside, and all the excitement that sprouts from our souls from living "down the shore."

One of my favorite features of that house on Mulberry was the linoleum floor area on the very end of the family room, leading out to the backyard through a sliding door. The reason I loved that floor and the four-foot cylindrical wooden stick that allowed that door to "lock" by stopping it, was performance. I was able to dance and slide around in my socks to whatever song I put the needle on from the family room record player. There's more though. What's the point of dancing if nobody's watching? The inner exhibitionist in me knew that our backyard neighbors could see in through the short green wire fence if they were in their yard. I'd dance for them. It was my first stage. I never felt embarrassed doing it. It is still hard to embarrass me. I think privacy is overrated. I mean, I'd never strip down to nothing in front of a crowd then *or* now, but I love the magic of performance, even if the audience is thinking *WTF*. In some ways, even better—I shocked them. I made them squirmy. It's no coincidence I am the biggest Madonna fan on Earth. Art should sometimes make us squirm.

I was born with drums in my bones, and those drums often found their exit in the space of my family room. If there was a song with a drum pattern that pounded in your chest like your best day or like a bowl of your favorite ice cream for breakfast, it was my song. Think The Knack's "My Sharona." According to my mother, I'd bounce and do squats with such ferocity that my diaper would fall off. The songs with drums that sent me to the moon is on an endless list and in several genres. If the song was designed to get you moving, it was my song. Synth drums, real drums, snare drums, bass drums—all of it gave me release. Right in the middle of my family room, out of the speakers, through my legs, rumbling straight through my nervous system to make a happy girl. There's a precise sensory regulation that comes with the beating and the vibration. It's so prominent that your body surrenders to it, then kind of heals itself. It's really tricky to explain. The more chaos you express out, the less chaos that remains in?

Against the left wall of our front family room was a wooden desk with drawers and handles that were brass and kind of rustic looking for the time. It was a statement piece as it had presence and gave that wall the feel of an English study. It was my favorite piece of furniture in the house for a long time. There was a lamp on it and anything we needed to write letters or work on a school assignment. I sat there every night and did my homework from fifth grade through high school, until I transitioned to my bedroom desk for more privacy. The desk made me feel important. At one point we even kept our fishbowl on top. That fish attempted suicide twice, diving to the carpet from the top of the desk. I remember being in eighth grade and having a ton of homework on trick or treat night (not Halloween because in my hometown they were two different nights because of the massive town Halloween parade). I spent hours happily completing my homework while answering the door in between tasks. I remember feeling grown up about the whole thing. That desk made homework feel a little more enjoyable. In the center was a day planner enclosed in a protector with faux leather edges.

In our family room we had a record player that I was allowed to control, unlike the very old Victrola in our living room that sat on a wooden chest above my dad's pipe collection. The record player was a plentiful source of joy for me. I collected close to two hundred records from ages six through thirteen. Every penny I had went toward music until I had a car to pay for. When I had to budget, my cassette collection suffered. One of the earliest records that got a ton of airtime in my family room was Dionne Warwick's *Heartbreaker*. Truthfully, it's so hard for me to listen to presently because without the warped nature of those keyboards, it just isn't the same.

When Hela Young appeared in our family room night after night, I felt safe, settled, and full of our dinner. I felt like anything was possible. Maybe Dad would win the Pick Six, and we could then add a basement with more space for toys, dancing, and friends. Maybe if my dad won the lottery, we could put air conditioners all over the house. Hela was hope.

Figure Skating

The scrapes of the blade on ice and the tight grip of concentration were the hooks for me. The part of the human spirit that's fiercest runs rampant in Olympic athletes, and I noticed it.

Here's how the figure skating three-dimensional fantasy of mine looked, starting that year when Katerina Witt found her way to my family room to the tune of "Carmen" during the Winter Olympics in Sarajevo. Her red costume, her dark eye shadow, and most of all, the champion in her eyes. I loved her. I wanted to be her. Athletic, feminine, and so skilled because of hours of hard work. Also, she looked like a very nice person.

I'd make sure I had socks on, and dancing tights and leotard. The music began, and without taking my eyes off the chunky screen, I'd glide around my own "ice" of a carpet, twist, turn, pull out every dance move I knew. Every extension of my leg and torso until it felt like I was the one competing. Every now and then, I'd pause just to watch her skate—the love and intensity in her eyes. I was on the way to the gold medal with her. I ended up watching every single skater that year, anxious to see the men's competition too. During the 2022 Beijing Olympics I could safely say that I have never missed the Winter Olympics Figure Skating Singles. Nothing against pairs. There's something more magical for me about a solo skate.

There have been so many favorites along the way. How did I choose a favorite? Just a gut feeling. Every time Carolina Kostner from Italy graced the ice, I couldn't help but smile and cheer for her success. Something in her eyes that is passionate and kind makes her a champion, in my opinion.

o

Watching figure skating was so much more than medals and being a champion for a kid like me. Even now as an adult, despite knowing more of the technical aspect and just how grueling of a sport it is. I saw through the glamour even as a kid, but here's what I truly saw—ice, fresh air, freedom, movement, grace, precision, and the sound of that thin metal blade moving a human body through time and space.

I used to wonder how each skater knew this was the event they'd like to devote every waking hour to. Like do young figure skaters always favor winter over summer? Are they also lovers of cold and refreshing over humidity and sunshine? The clarity of the routines—the moves that become so engrained in a brain each time the song begins—these were all things I could relate to at a young age because of dancing school and my tendency to love a regimen and predictability of actions. To know that when the drums kick in, I was over here on this part of the stage, but then when the cello solo arrives, I am lined up with Lisa or Jill.

Oh, and then my favorite part right before that last count of eight—oh how I love that part when my right leg got to look like a perfect line. More than the sensations in my body during the specific moves and chunks of the routine, was the overall routine itself. The sensory regulation that accompanies getting a routine down is indescribable for me. Mastering a set of steps over multiple sets of counts—even in orchestra or band—it's the stuff that let me sleep at night.

Bubble Gum Debra

I remember when my brother and I were too young to stay alone for my parents' date nights, so my mom would hire local teenage babysitters—circa 1986. That puts me in fourth grade. One random neighborhood girl with poofy hair and the jean-sweater combo was named Debra. She became our favorite because she brought us brand-name candy. But more than the Whatchamacallits or Twix bars, it was the Bubblicious Strawberry or the Hubba Bubba Grape that set my soul on fire. She introduced me to real bubble gum. This was a rite of passage. Debra dealt me the good stuff, and so how could I possibly go back to mediocre chewing gum?

My mom only bought Carefree sugarless as a rule. I never realized how shitty those bubbles were until I had a comparison. Enter the sugar-filled dream cubes known as Bubblicious and Hubba Bubba. Rectangular truth.

Thanks to Debra, my taste for gum became lethal. The jaw action, essential. Another habit for my very sensory young self to rely on for some pressure relief. That initial explosion of sweetness and the fresh pounding of the molars onto this scientific miracle known as bubblegum. It was a spiritual experience in those initial seconds, up until the large bubbles that could form, then remove from your mouth carefully while holding the part in your teeth. I don't chew gum much anymore because of my TMJ, but what I wouldn't pay for the original pack of Hubba Bubba Grape or Bubbilicous Strawberry. To feel it between my upper and lower chompers like a tough piece of pink elastic, clamping something definitive and squelchy for the ultimate pressure relief. In circles, repeatedly. I chewed a ton of gum growing up.

When I was seven my mom had to cut my hair short because I blew a huge bubble in the shower. Water and gum make for hair disasters. I didn't care. It was worth every chew. Sometimes I'd mold the thick piece of gum and pretend I had braces.

I did some research about bubblegum and its juicy roots. According to the Candy Funhouse blog written about bubblegum by Joey Hejazi in September of 2021, it was invented in 1928 as a flub. It was supposed to be a batch of typical chewing gum, but Walter Diemer made a less sticky batch and it became bubblegum. The blog was oozing with good information—pink was the original color because it's the color most natural to factory usage. Rain-Blo changed things in 1941 when they began matching colors to flavors. One thing I enjoyed reading was that chewing bubblegum has been proven to reduce muscle tension and improve focus on tasks. That made me feel seen. It's a total lie that gum stays in your gut for seven years. It cannot be broken down, but you can poop it out, and you will.

I dug deeper and researched the two brands that I favored—Bubbilicious and Hubba Bubba. The first launched into the world in 1977 just like me; Hubba Bubba came two years later, as a baby of Wrigley. Labels evolved through years, as did flavors and graphics. I hold the early 1980s wrapper near to my heart, when Debra gave us the goods.

Gum is so nostalgic for so many of us, I think. Big League Chew at the Little League fields. Popping a slice of Juicy Fruit in just for a palette cleanse, only to have it fade into bullshit plain elastic within minutes. Taking your gum out before a kiss. Chewing gum to cut your nerves. The cheap hard sticks of gum that would come with some trading cards.

For me, I will always remember Debra, the teenage babysitter who brought the superior sugar product into my life, straight through my sensory needles and knobs.

Age Twelve

One minute I was this white Italian-American girl with a plethora of Jewish, Polish, and Italian friends, and the next, a seventh grader with a handful of Black friends who got a kick out of my goofball ways and my interest in them. I wanted to know more about their lives. The brown shades of their of skin looked so beautiful to me, and their ability to laugh out loud at just about anything were interesting to a girl from an all-white neighborhood with friends of similar home economies. Dinner times. Homework spaces. Where everyone has fair shares. I never saw divides like this before seventh grade.

You might be thinking—*how do you know they didn't have fair shares? You're assuming a lot about their lives.* But I'm not. I paid attention to the things that made me draw these conclusions. I'm speaking from a place of awareness. We had zero talk about race. We had zero talk about anything related to race. It was 1989. I didn't know that it was not appropriate to be interested in them just for the color of their skin. And that's only half true. Meaning, it wasn't just their differences. It was their energy.

I finally had Black friends, and it made me sad that life took so long to show me truths like this—that kids need friends of different color, different religions, different values. It balances us and builds acceptance and tolerance. I mean, duh. Life waits sometimes to show us the light, and it's annoying. In addition to finally having four Black friends who expressed themselves jubilantly in between changing classes and with a spark of personality I craved, I had Amanda Anello. Amanda was white and Italian like me and knew Tyree, Tori, Andrea, and Danielle long before I did. They all went to elementary school together, and you could hear their warm, cozy, street jargon from South Toms River where they all lived. And I didn't have the right to imitate or join in just yet. I wanted it though. I'd listen intently to the way they made fun of each other lovingly, or called each other out, and I felt so jealous. The bonds were clear, and I wanted in.

Amanda showed me that she too was very Italian-American with the talk of her mom's lasagna and dad's relatives from Newark, but unlike me she didn't lack common sense or street smarts when someone threatened to beat someone up by the lockers. Amanda knew that not everybody was dished equal points or snacks or outfit options for the week. Amanda was sort of like Leather Tuscadero, and I was Jenny Piccolo and I was uncomfortable with the strength of that contrast, so I made every effort to change it up a little. I listened and learned. "Girl. You hafta loosen up a little."

Amanda taught me how she took a sewing needle or a safety pin and gently carved the shape of a cross in this side of her thumb to create a scar in that shape. I was too chicken to go deep enough to get that scar though. I tried. I never could do it, like the way I feared jumping back into the handspring only a couple of years before. I'm making Amanda sound so bad-ass when she was just as loving and gentle as anyone I'd befriended in my life. A goofy giggle and sweet disposition. Huge hair, but we all had that. Her edge was peaceful, but fiercely present. She wore more black and denim than me, and she proceeded with kids she didn't know more cautiously. She had bigger boundaries—something I'd never witnessed before.

The way Amanda spoke to me was different than the way she spoke to our Black friends, and it went beyond the vocabulary. It had a rhythm. Sometimes they'd skip verbs like *is* and *are* and kept their sentences briefer, and I ate it up like pasta. Their bonds were born in kindergarten. The loyalty to each other was amazing, and I only saw those bonds with the south part of our town.

I felt like the outsider. I had to earn the insider status. I had to earn the trust of the kids from the south side of town at twelve years old. I loved the challenge, and I adored them. The boisterous laughter, the roars of middle school nonsense, and the sound of their true selves. I remember them. I remember Amanda. To this day. Because one minute I was a white Italian-American girl with only friends of the same color, and the next, someone who hated those limits and those fences. I'd never go back to being the same again. I'd have friends of all races, colors, genders, and polka dots for the rest of my life. The things Amanda got to do first. I listened and learned.

Stars in My Mouth

A month away from graduating high school, I met someone very special from the high school across Toms River, closer to the river and closer to salvation. I met Chris in May of 1995 of my senior year— it was his senior year too, but from the high school on the south side of town (see above). Chris hung out with passionate people with street smarts, common sense, and he had Black friends. Their high school was more diverse, and it made my heart flop—in the good way that sensed it was phenomenal, and in the gross way, knowing my end of town was so ... very ... homogenous. What could we learn when we all looked and grew up the same? Not enough. This was 1995.

We started dating. Before Chris, I'd dated Gregg for many years. My first love. Gregg and I played sports in sync, marched with our baritone horns in sync, and loved each other very much in sync. Then I got antsy, he got jealous over everything, and the boat sunk. We broke up. Which meant my friendships in that circle shifted, bobbled, and broke apart a little bit, so I took a hard right turn and connected with other friends, leading me to Chris.

Chris didn't come from much, so he loved what sparkled in the way of natural beauty and what was possible on the grass, in the sand, and the dirt under the sky. He showed me the night stars so vividly that I could taste them in the back of my throat. Really that was his sweet saliva, but the surreal nature of those nights made anything possible. Our dates were comprised of these secret shore town locations, and now that I look back—we were totally trespassing on people's lawns in Island Heights that summer. It was dark, so no one caught us. Those home-owners probably drunk on Brandy. We'd lie on our backs, on the vitamin-scented soil, and swallow the stars over the bay. And I thought, is this guy for real? *He was.* Realer than anyone I'd ever known.

His side of the tracks was ten times better because on that side of the track they seek the stars, the earth, the salt. I never really bothered to look at the sky until him. The summer of 1995, my last official summer living at home, was when I finally understood the beauty of where we lived. The summer I realized it was perfectly suited to my sensory regulation issues, and if I focused on his breath, his voice, my breath, his smell, I really could taste the stars.

"Isn't it cool?" He'd ask me.

"Yes." I thought I was dreaming sometimes, the way he admired the sky and the free, open air. Even then it had occurred to me that he must've craved something bigger than him because maybe he carried old pain and cycles of trauma. He knew that plastic and metal things didn't matter. He knew that all that mattered was humanity and our planet.

He never cared about identifying constellations or planets. His only concern the visceral. The feeling your body and skin get from sacred silence under a navy-blue sky.

When I kissed him it was different than my first love. Not better or worse. More about the act of the kiss—the desperation, the connection, and the craving to be understood. Like the stars we ate. I didn't feel the same way it did with my first love, but I knew it was because he couldn't. My first boyfriend loved me, yes, but he loved himself first, which is another lesson I learned from him. You really must accept who you are to live within your own walls, yourself. Chris was way ahead of us all, spiritually. The "other side of the tracks" had so much to teach us.

Chris's gift for relating to people and conversation expanded my own appreciation for both. He'd meet my friends up at Rider University on the weekends, and they'd become his friends. He was a powerful listener and was intrigued by their interests and pursuits, whether it was music, weed, or politics. He'd engage with his entire self, the same way I did with him in silence under lemon-yellow sunshine back home, or the diamond-like stars in the strangers' yards.

One time, he showed me how to really go to the beach. All you needed was a pair of legs, a smile, and a sprint into the ocean fully clothed. If it was 4 p.m. on a random Wednesday, even better. We'd dash into the waves before sunset, then dry off the old-fashioned way in the salt air or in the car on the way over the bridge. He didn't fuss over wet car seats or sand on the dashboard.

One time we spent a lazy July afternoon on the creek in a hidden treasure called Double Trouble Park. I have no idea where he obtained the black tube, but he found one, and we drifted in the hot sun, in around a million mosquito clusters and overgrowth. I remember vines, leaves, plant life, and sweltering heat. I remember being so into him, that none of that mattered. He had it so bad for nature, and in turn, I had it so bad for him. Nature didn't disappoint him, and it was like he sought its free, unconditional embrace, sharing it all with his new girlfriend from the snobby side of town.

I never suspected these rendezvous would change my perspective forever—the way I continue to praise the pine trees in winter and kiss the marigolds that endure the summer storms. I loved nature as a young child too, but he reminded me to keep loving it after I'd been wrapped up in competing for my grades, my music, and my social status. I don't recall much about our intimacy with the exception of his mouth. He always tasted like watermelon and cigarettes. We dated for my first fifteen months in college, then went our separate ways peacefully.

I mostly only remember our spiritual jaunts and conversations about who we wanted to be in life. He put stars in my mouth.

We Work with Our Hands

I know the beauty marks on my mom's hands by heart. There was one that at six years old, in my opinion, enveloped her name: *Corinna.* It sat at the wrinkly part of the wrist, on the outer edge just below that bone that is round and ball-sockety. It is light brown and asymmetrical, and it just felt pretty to my eyes as a child. I know it sounds weird, but sometimes those freckles and beauty marks carry a comfort about them. I think maybe because they represent imperfection. Authentically human and flawed.

My mom's hands are one of her most memorable features, though she will tell you, as I will too, since mine are similar, that they're short and stubby. Our fingers might not be compared to ballerina fingers of other women, but they've done things. We've created, sliced, chopped, scrubbed, twisted, untangled, and molded things. I think that's worth the look it leaves on your skin at the end. My mom has a way with textiles. She can touch a skirt from Boscov's or Macys and tell you if it's made well. If you give her a few yards of a nice cotton fabric, she'll make you curtains, or in my case, at eight years old, a special witch's robe for Halloween. It was black with small pumpkins all over it and cinched at the waist with an orange silky rope.

My mom touches fabrics like they're precious, even if it's a skirt from Marshalls. She understands and honors what it took to create each piece, having gone to school for fashion merchandising at LIM in New York City. She hemmed pants with precision. A pattern strikes her as a "must have," and her sewing machine is her typewriter—sewing together cloth stories like my witch robe, my gypsy dress, my brother's pirate costume, my sweater with a giant poofy E, and on and on. She takes things around my house still—pillows that I've attempted to hand sew but couldn't quite close tight enough. She runs it across the machine for that reinforcement stitch.

Squish Squish

I believe in the folds of my heart and soul that the medium I didn't have enough of as a child was modeling clay. I don't think I had the awareness to identify the need, either. I had piles of crayons, boxes of markers, stacks of coloring books, and so many scraps of fabric, but none quite targeted what was going on with my excess energy and need for input. I guess if I knew to request a moldable medium like clay, I might have done that, then I'd have been able to find calm and focus. The difficult task required by my fingers with clay might have quelled impulses to gnaw on my fingernails. The clay might have kept my hands out of my mouth, but I can never be one hundred percent sure. To my mom and dad's credit, they enrolled me in sports, arts, and camps to keep my body and hands engaged.

I wonder if therapy dough had even existed in the 1980s if they would have known to give me a tin? Or maybe I would've spotted it myself in a store like Pandemonium or Caldor. I'd have thrived with the slicing, bending, pressing, and rolling. If it smelled like lemons or oranges, that would've been a bonus to my nose too. It might have engaged with my early sensory puzzle, decades prior to finding solace in Reiki and breathing. I imagine this for seven-year-old me—a liberal chunk of turquoise modeling clay that I could've kept in a small Tupperware. I'd remove the chunk as I needed it. Maybe we'd be driving up the parkway towards Westfield or waiting in line at Bamberger's. Maybe we'd be in JCPenney's in December when they jack the heat up to eighty. That clay might've slapped me out of my state of dysregulation faster than you can say "It's hot in here!"

ABCs

I often wonder if I knew how to keep my systems in check and regulate my nervous system in my childhood, if my life path and choices would've been the same? I often wonder if my art would suffer now as an adult if I didn't *require* it to soothe me. I will never know the answer, so all I can do is reflect and use it in the content of my art to connect to others. Maybe inform others. Relate to others.

As part of satisfying my undying need for arrays and structures that have a clear beginning, middle, and end, I've spelled out an abecedarian. Again, I can only come at it from my own shoes.

A

Arm hair presence is strong for the five- through ten-year-old on the beach or outdoors from 7 a.m. until 7 p.m. daily. It smells of sun, sweat, and the concrete of the neighborhood, and the sensory-driven kid knows because she sniffs. This will continue throughout the summers, and locales affect the smell—salty element or the rocks and gravel element involved in hours of bike riding.

Arm hair is the thing to be hidden from ages ten through sixteen, when it bothers her so much. Even though she has friends with much thicker and darker strands and from wrist to shoulder, it bothers her. Just that small little patch of light brown Italian-ness is enough to make her panic in the group of hairless blondes. So many techniques to disguise it, hide it, distract from it. Her society tells her it's ugly.

Arm hair is ripped vigorously from its roots the fall of senior year when the teenager realizes this is a thing that can be done with a super stinky creme called *Nair.* And girl happily realizes that only after a year of using this cream, the hair just stops growing and it's never a nuisance again. Some cultures cherish and celebrate hair all over the body. She can't braid that into her brain. She tried. She can't. It doesn't ever faze her when other women have it, but her own arms? The sensory dysregulation surrounding this is too much to handle.

B

Biting fingernails and all that comes with that lifelong struggle. It becomes a management system like any other bad habit. Along the way, it also became married with smell, as the cuticles love to hold the scent of fresh garlic and olive oil for days, even after a strong shower. When you waited tables in college, one of your tasks was to prepare the dressing bottles—refill the oil into their small dispensers—you know the ones—the cone shaped metal tops that sit in this little holder's slot, opposite of the red wine vinegar. By the time your nails got rid of the oil smell, it was your weekly shift again.

C

Cracking of air pockets in between your vertebrae is an essential for the human who likes things pulled, prodded, dug into, and adjusted. Even more advanced, the sound, the vibration, and the psychological satisfaction of hearing vertebrae pop back to where they belong. All systems clicking back into place so that the human body is given the stage to work to the best of her ability.

You discovered it in Mr. Greenfield's history class, Junior year, you think? If you lower your back gently, sliding down your spine, you can pop things yourself. Then in college you can get your strong and coordinated friends to apply loving force between your shoulders on an exhale, and it's popcorn central. Then when you're in your forties, you watch Dr. Tubio work his head cradle on patients on Instagram "alleviating years of pain" from a swift and loud neck adjustment. The ripple of the bones snapping back where they belong.

D

Dry lip avoidance becomes a part time job. Just ask your steeple-shaped lipsticks. Those stray rough shreds of chapped lip will never grace your mouth. Your lips never get the chance to go that dry, but it's also sort of become about the colors, as you cannot tell a lie. Coffees, plums, the occasional peach. The dryness creates a discomfort in mood though. Chapsticks need not apply as they offer no beauty sport option.

E

Electric as the avenue. It must be regulated very carefully within. If you drink anything with alcohol within two hours of bedtime, your entire body feels like it's been plugged into an outlet, ready for maximum engagement. It's especially detrimental on a family vacation when you're supposed to be relaxed and leisurely, but since Mommy can't sleep, she puts everyone on high alert, and it overall sucks. One time, you even hit day three of no sleep and your body decided in the middle of lunch at a quiet diner in Vermont was the time to shake like a leaf uncontrollably while you faked being *fine*. "Mommy is just cold. Don't worry."

Intense shivering can be a nervous system response. A panic attack in your body, though in your mind, you feel at ease. In your mind, you have talked yourself down to serene to just make it to evening when you can try again to sleep. But your body is like "Nope." You've had enough, and you are breaking down into these segments of scary, shivery panic. So how did you shake that bodily earthquake out in the middle of the quiet Vermont diner, as your oldest child cries when you can't stop shaking violently? You excused yourself from the table and sprinted outside in the cold rain until your body was done with its earthquake.

F

Full moons charge the system. You notice your sleep is disturbed, but also that your hope is high when the moon is full. You notice your gastro system is healthiest during the big white ball in her most opulent dress. You notice your girls and their sleep affected too when lunar lady gets to her roundest, plumpest, most virtuous viewing. Your mom will call the house after dinner, "Girls! Go look out the window! Look at the moon." Like it's an ancestral thing with women. You know moon is your original mom, you swear it. First her, then trees, then humans. This gorgeous chain of rock-solid moms.

G

Green is a comfort zone. So is gray. Unless it settles heavy in your eyelids. Green means summer grass, celery, and escarole. Green means spearmint leaves in your mom's homemade iced tea and the chunky green crayon in the kindergarten crayon box. Green means Christmas and string beans swimming in oil and vinegar, barely boiled. When given the choice of ice pops in a classic squeeze-pop situation you go green for lime. Green for sour apple Jolly Rancher. Green for fresh spinach salads covered in chunks of fennel and lobster. Green for go.

H

Hot. Too hot. Heat. NEVER.

I

Itchy wool and fringy fabrics create drama in the eyes, ears, throat, and mind. Tags must be cut off by your mother. But that faded away in adulthood.

One of your earliest memories of itchy wool and things like it, kind of breaks your heart. Your precious Grandma Josephine, more commonly known as Grandma Jo, used to crochet beautiful blankets and quilts. For your brother and you, for her children—your dad, your aunt Connie and their much younger brother, Uncle Tony. She'd choose one to three colors for each quilt and create a sort of chevron pattern. But the yarn she used. You can almost hear and feel it scratching in your ears and mouth. As if you were biting it for the first time.

Your quilt was a lilac purple and white, and brother's a navy, white, and fire-engine red. You kept them draped on the foot board of your beds at home, or on top of the comforter. It never touched your body because if it did, you'd itch for hours at the squeaky scratch of the wool. Despite its main ingredient being the purest love from beautiful Grandma Jo.

Those quilts graced your families' homes in oranges, golds, browns, blues, yellows, mint greens—so soft from afar, so dangerously anxiety-inducing up close. Instead of your own body, you learned to wrap your dolls in their well-intentioned love.

J

Jelly shoes weren't really shoes, but rather torture devices on a beautiful and breezy summer night on the shrimpy, sausagy boardwalk. They pinched every piece of soft skin on their victims' feet.

K

Kindergarten crayons: plump, square, or cylindrical. Coloring in coloring books with everything you've got. Coloring away the days to express yourself and feel the delight of being alive.

L

Lemons save your life all-around. Vitamin C shooting out into ice cubes or over fish, pasta, or apples to keep them from browning. Summer in a bowl when left whole and on display. Lemon trees as aromatic queens.

M

Melted wax, melted chocolate, melted cheese. Once cooled down, do these textures need any more explanation?

N

Necks being adjusted. Nectarines in season. Nail polish dripped onto canvas in swizzles and perfect circles like it's 1987 again.

O

Over Stimulation: see holiday gatherings, birthday parties, graduation parties, long car rides, Disney World, and hot department stores around the holidays.

P

Playdough. Make it, buy it. Cut it.

Q

Quell of winter cold against your bare, hungry face that dreams of hot chocolate by the fire with your soft dog.

R

Red in a bedroom is a hard no.
On the lip, soft yes.

S

Smells as Satan and saints—the dichotomy. It all depends on the day and season.

T

Talk to me after you've eaten an apple or brushed your teeth. I don't want to smell your stinky breath.

U

Understanding: underwear must be the granny variety seventy percent of the time. They keep everything in place, hug your parts with their unconditional cotton, like a favorite pillow, and they coat your parts for what's certain to be a sweaty, successful day in the sunshine or snow.

V

Vacation suitcase essentials matter to the sensory person. The following items have saved your vacations, many times over: a small floor fan for the hotel room, which also serves as a sound machine, a tube or container of Aquaphor for under the nose so that the carpet dust doesn't jump up your nostrils and make your head hurt all day. A twenty-four-pack of water for a family of four because hydration is key all the time for the sensory you. Constant flushing of the physical and psychological kind. Sensory-*you* thinks she can flush away a headache, and sometimes she can. The last essential item for a vacation is instant coffee. You like to wake up before anyone else and pour hot water from the tiny kettle and make yourself a cup of organic instant coffee to sip in the dark. It starts your day in peace and quiet and with the dose of caffeine you need to feel alive before your hustle to keep your kids alive begins. Also, so you can poop before you leave the house.

W

Windows are your best friend in the world of sensory processing. Windows lead to outdoors. Outdoors is fresh air. Fresh air can contrast the stuffy in the doctor's office or the concert hall or the stale smoke-filled kitchen of your friend's aunt's house in grubby towns or mistaken locations. How did I get here? And now I need to get out.

Bonus: Weighted blankets. Get one.

X

X marks the knots in your shoulder being dug out by a paleontologist disguised as a trained massage therapist, chiropractor, or partner with skilled elbows and thumbs. The people in your life who know exactly how to find the knot, press the knot, wait there until it hurts so good, sort of thing, like an overall surface area of tension before they repeat the process again.

Y

Yelling helps sometimes. Don't yell at someone. Yell with them or into your favorite forest.

Z

Zippers in pants are evil now. We have enough to worry about daily than whether we will reach the top part of the pants with a zipper. Why not let our pants bend to our needs with a nice, hidden elastic waist band on all clothes. This way, the pant-wearer feels his/her/their freedom to maybe eat both halves of the tuna on rye or maybe order that small brownie on a Friday after lunch? Zippers are yet one extra way we can't live our lives to the fullest while still being responsible around the donuts. Maybe one day we want a donut. The zipper disagrees, and I disagree with the duty of those metal teeth being chased up the gut.

Pre-Game Shapes and Colors

Colorful pencils spread over white paper. That was my personal pre-party in my dorm room throughout four years at Rider University. At the time I didn't realize it, but I suspect it was some sort of sacred meditation prior to joining in with sorority crowds, drinking crowds, and the wonderfully welcoming weed-worshipping crowds.

In his memoir, Dave Grohl talks about song writing and music session rituals that artists throughout history have developed, including himself. I'm not comparing myself to them. Okay, I am. Even though I wasn't prepping to make award-winning music, I was prepping my entire self for the energy I didn't always cope well in, especially when tossed in large amounts: "Hey Elaina! Come here! Look at this! Have another! Don't you love my party girl/guy vibe so much? EEK! AAK! Bleek! Bloook!" You get the idea.

I'd turn up my music, sit at my desk, and draw—shapes, florals, vines, trains, ovals, and hearts. I'd use either pencils or thin sharpie markers, then I'd color the interiors of these objects so hard with my twenty-four brightly colored pencils. From soft periwinkles to peanut butter browns. There was a candle flickering on my wooden desk, a definite violation of dorm living, and dim lighting from the faint ceiling light.

My beautiful roommate Amy would scurry in and out of our room, flat iron plugged in, and our door often slightly propped open. If it was a Friday, there was a ton of activity in the dorm hallway—people preparing to go home for the weekend, or the opposite—people like Amy and me, settling in for the weekend with our choice of social gatherings on campus with people we liked. Or people with parties. But obviously, for me, it took mental preparation, and it wasn't because I found the parties toxic or anything like that. It was more complex for me. It was the stimulus. Way too much of it to dive into head-first.

Similar to high school, I never felt like I fit into any one social hive, but I was friends with all of them, and I genuinely adored all of them. At Rider University I was friends with the theater students, the athletes, the Greek communities, the self-proclaimed stoners, and the laid-back beer pongers, guitar-playing Kerouacs, which included my best friends at the time. Like high school, all these groups tended to emit noise in their own way. I liked loud. I liked people. Yet, there was still a giant chunk of me that required a spiritual sort of ceremony to prepare myself for the hullabaloo.

I'd sit at my dorm desk, makeup perfect, stomach flat, outfit *fire*, music faint, candle lit, and I'd sketch. I have a very specific memory of pressing play on Natalie Merchant's *Ophelia* album in the fall of 1998. My musical choices for sacred ceremony of preparation were often the antithesis of how the rest of the night would feel. Looking back, I believe it was my way of grounding myself before I even knew what grounding meant. The opening track, called "Ophelia" is soulful, ethereal, and of another era, much like most of Natalie's music. I'd draw long thin vines or hundreds of circles connected. What was I conjuring exactly? Nothing or something? I really don't know, but I do know that

I always found myself fighting between staying in my room or leaving for the parties that bursted "WOOT WOOTs." I knew deep down that staying alone all night would make me miserable because I genuinely liked people and loud music and hard dancing. The struggle I think came from also loving my solace. I cannot imagine other college creatives didn't have their own rituals, and I'd put money on it that many never found it in themselves to leave that inside space. I imagine many said, "Fuck it," and stayed where they were with their markers, paint, weed, and vocalists on CD. I never had my own weed—in fact, of the half dozen times I've smoked, I wasn't on campus. I've been riverside, other campuses, houses, and backyards. Maybe my sketches were *my* weed.

The more I reflect, the more I see how connected it is to my sensory stuff. It was a way of seeking input the way some kids need a fidget spinner or a stress ball. I'd also compare it to stretching before a run. Pressing the colored pencils into the precise shapes I'd sketch gave me a deep satisfaction and unblocked my mind and heart before I threw myself to the wilderness—whether that meant a frat house dance floor, a dorm suite steeping in pot fumes, or a room crowded with hippies and army boot wearing crop-top girls like myself. If I wasn't seeing anyone at the time, these candle-lit-art rituals were even longer. If I was seeing someone, I wasn't as anxious inside. I knew I had a safety zone to mush my face into—meaning his chest or face. I am a true mix of introvert and extrovert, the first one being incrementally more powerful. But if I leaned too far into the introversion, I'd likely never escape. It was and still is, a fine line for me.

As a forty-something, when my family and I vacation, I crave downtime before our evening "up-time." It consists of a shower, the hotel bathrobe, reruns on the Food Network, and rest. I need to decompress prior to our evenings full of dinner, walking, ice cream, and maybe fireworks. Thankfully, the hubby is the same way. If he wasn't there'd be collisions and life wouldn't be so grand.

Sensory Processing Disorder

I love science. I believe in science. I honor science. Science explains most of my weird habits that aren't so weird after all. The nervous system is very important. Like, mega important. It's responsible for how we perceive the world around us. It's responsible for decisions we make. Others can sometimes mistake the sensory person as being rude, or worse, "high maintenance."

For example, it's the summer of 1985, and my family and I are waiting in a very long line at the Old Tyme Tavern. The wait is supposed to be an hour long, and we must wait in a narrow hallway where the room is limited and the people are plentiful. My body is telling me to find something hard to lean on so that I can stretch and twist. The people around me simply think, "Ugh, this kid. She can't sit still. She's misbehaving and whiny."

According to *Helping Your Child with Sensory Regulation* by Suzanne Mouton-Odum, our nervous system detects imbalances in our environment, then seeks to correct the imbalance with other behaviors. One of the first things I thought of was this: I'm in a crowded coffeehouse. It's hot. The coffee bean smell is overpowering and I'm nowhere near the door. What do I do when my nervous system is on fire with its detection of these imbalances? I race to the restroom, run the cold water on my hands and take deep breaths. I might even splash the back of my neck, grab my lemon essential oil from my tote bag and sniff it for a beat. I'd talk myself back into returning to the uncomfortable temperature and overpowering aromas of the coffeehouse. I've grown more elegant about it over the years, using breath techniques that are less frantic and more controlled.

The author talks about overstimulation and under-stimulation. I must've bitten down on items because my nervous system was under-stimulated or maybe I have it backwards. Either way, something inside me had to correct the scenario I found myself in while in the backseat of my mom's green Buick station wagon. I bit into the headset for comfort and stimulation. I was feeling dysregulated.

Some kids have an over-response to smell, and others, the opposite. I would've been classified as the first one. Which brings me to my dad's green tree air freshener. I had a real over response to that dangling piece of chemically treated paper. The research indicates that in a situation like that, it would've helped me if I had an even stronger smell in my reach to stuff my nose into for relief. It had to have been the open window. I had to have rolled it down, only to have been told to roll it right back up again. It makes me wonder if that tree was my dad's pleasant smell. Maybe he liked those trees because he had been an under-responder of smell and that tree was his form of comfort?

The part of the research I found particularly relatable was the mention of visual clutter, and how it can create anxiety and disruption to the nervous system. It's exactly what it sounds like: stuff everywhere, sending the individual into anything from panic to withdrawal from the setting. When my first child was born, you can imagine the emotions running wild in our families—first grandchild and first baby among friends. These emotions meant that when I returned home from the hospital with her, our house would be filled with gift bags, relatives, and packages. It sent a new mom (me) over the edge, having to deal with these items covering my house, along with being a new mother. Toss in sleep deprivation and my physical pain, and you have a woman in a very wobbly state. The clutter in my home, though thoughtful and celebratory, was too much for me to handle. Thankfully, I have a supportive spouse who helped mitigate, and a mother who spent the night so I could retreat into some much-needed sleep. My best advice for new mothers is some space and spread out the visits and gifts. Sensory dysregulation or not, I think these boundaries need to be established. We know you are so excited to spend time with the new baby but give it a few days. Sometimes moms have war wounds, both physically and mentally.

A truly dynamic line in this research was this line: "Celebrate your child's unique nervous system." The sections proceed to discuss how no shame should be attached to your child's individual needs when they feel dysregulated. Give them the accommodations they need so that they feel supported and able to carry on with their day. The accommodations will both strengthen your relationship with them and show them that they don't have to develop fear over new situations. Even as an adult I sometimes panic before a new event, wondering if I will be able to manage any unwanted stimuli, then having to make up excuses about why I "don't feel great" or how I "have to leave at a certain time." I am not angry with my parents because again, it wasn't something talked about or even known, so I cannot fault them. I got by okay, and it's certainly a lifelong management system no matter what.

Olfactory De-Mystified

Smell has eternally baffled scientists for decades. I spent all of August, September, and October of 2021 feverishly researching the sense with vigor. Like obsessive energy. That's how connected I felt to its science, knowing it's affected me since childhood. A.S. Barwich calls smell the Cinderella of the Senses in her book *Smellosophy.*

Certain smells have been labeled the champions of scent because of their strength of molecule and structure, which really means we can smell it, know it, identify it, and it lives. Those champion smells, according to one source are: lavender, lemon, baked cookies, cinnamon, and peppermint. The scent known to serve a purpose like relaxation is chamomile, whereas the scents to wake us up are rose and clove. Did you know that many scientists have learned that we've been conditioned as a society to be repulsed and disgusted by certain smells? In other words, we've been "told" what not to like. Apparently, until the 1620s, literature and poems show how people "delighted" in excretia. Basically, people didn't mind the smell of their own poop, pee, and sweat. I know. Obviously, things changed as decades progressed because we don't generally delight in these smells any longer. I mean, I speak for myself of course, but I imagine many of you will agree.

Right about here, I could ramble on for pages about odor prisms, classifications, semantic profiling of smells, and perception of smells. I could describe the biological process of smell in detail and tell you all about the 1998 analysis of fart smells, or I could drone on about how sickness can be smelled through breath and skin pores, but it's really not that kind of book. Now that you know these terms, you can type it all into your search bar in your own time.

In ancient India, oils were used to "breathe in goodness," which is a foundation in Ayurevedic culture. It assumes there is a cleansing nature to the oils, allowing the sniffer to experience renewal. Personally, I love that idea as part of a larger picture of starting fresh with each new day and experience.

The most relatable aspect of olfactory experiences, in my opinion, is the link to our memories. In August of 2012, mere months before Hurricane Sandy ravaged my hometown and many others on the coast, my mom was diagnosed with Non-Hodgkin's Lymphoma. Upon learning the kind she had—meaning the stage and pace at which it was predicted to progress, I forced myself into a very serious meditative state with my rosary beads. During this set of weeks leading up to knowing more information about her diagnosis, I'd make myself a nightly bath using pine-scented bubbles and a few drops of pine tree oil. I'd sink into the space with my rosary beads on the edge of the large tub. My Virgin Mary prayer card sat upright against the knob of the tub. I'd sit in the water, pray, and breathe. I asked the Mother Mary to protect my mom and not take her from me too soon. From my oldest child and from the second daughter I didn't yet have. I asked and asked and asked. I inhaled the smell of pine. I dreamed of years with my mom. As I type this it's been over ten successful years later. My mom is well. Healthier than most people her age, in fact. She will always have the Non-Hodgkin's, but it remains low and inactive in any way that shapes her daily life. I'm so grateful. I associate pine smells with this period of my life, with winter, my favorite season, and with renewal. It's always the scent I turn to when I seek refuge and hope. Of course, it has a Christmas energy about it, but it's so much more for me now.

Fruity Candy

When I was about fifteen years old, our neighbor next door had given us several pounds of starburst in the form of bags, in which the candies were individually wrapped. Jim Bowlby worked many years for a candy distributor. One summer, they let him keep a surplus of Starburst in two-pound bags. He gave us about four bags. That's eight pounds of juicy-fruit squares in our possession. My mom stored them in her dining room hutch. Little by little we whittled away at the candies—after dinner, after lunch, before dinner, before lunch. You name it. Nobody protested. That dining room hutch still, after thirty-plus years, has the lingering smell of sugary sweetness in the tones of lemon and orange. It's like the smell is its own new blended flavor of Starburst. It's faint, but it's there. Every time I go to my parents' house, and if I remember, I open that cabinet door to get a whiff of that year we ate all the candy. Though there's no concrete memory attached to Starburst, there's the dining room hutch wood smell too. I suppose if I think back hard enough I can remember those days as a teenager when my metabolism was on fire and sugar burned in seconds. If I think back hard enough, I can remember the generosity of our neighbors to give us this kind of stash. I never ever craved a Starburst again after that.

Hot Cars

I'm seven years old. I sit in the car with my parents in traffic on a late morning in June. The bridge toward the beach is backed up for miles. The air conditioning is broken, so my mom urges us to manually roll down the station wagon windows. I smell black tar, fishy guts, and sunshine. My head starts pounding, and I recognize in this moment of traffic jam that if I don't pull myself out of this, I'm kind of doomed to throw up and ruin my day before it begins. It's tough for me to remember my exact thought process on how to rescue myself, but I do know I looked for anything cool to touch. If there was nothing, I'd hang my face on the car door and wish upon a star that the traffic started moving. If not, I'd have to throw up outside the door or ask my mom for the water jug early.

Shower Soap

I'm twenty years old. I turn the knob on the shower of the dorm hallway bathroom where we shower. There are maybe three other girls showering and so the cohesion becomes lemon, passionfruit, and maybe a vanilla bean. Our poofs soaked in their individual essences. Ones we've chosen to represent ourselves. What scent do we want our friends to associate with us? The shaving creams enter the scene, and nothing is cohesive nor attached in a lineage anymore. The scents beat each other up, and not one is discernible anymore. They fight, and I wince.

Coffee and Wood

I'm forty-four years old. I enter the kitchen of The Mermaid Inn in Mystic Connecticut and I smell the bones of an old house in Newark where my grandmother lived in the 1980s. The wood. The stone. I remember pasta and butter in bowls, and how that smell married in so nicely with the wood and stone. I remember my grandmother's Sanka instant coffee smell, soft and moderate. I loved our trip to Connecticut, needless to say.

Smooth Boys

I've dated my share of smooth guys. The guys who despise hair on legs, arms, and face as much as I do. I learned early on that I *like* hair on guys. Nevertheless, I was in my early twenties, and it was all fine by me—hair or no hair—until I discovered the symbolism of the smooth guy. The reason I don't like smooth guys is simple: it meant I had to stay smoother or as smooth as them. It's exhausting ... but like all other dating, it's a journey in bumpy, anarchic humanity. Why do we prefer things we prefer? What is it about these little hair details that send me over the edge?

I'm going to break it down. Why I *don't* love the shiny smoothness when it comes to men, chapter one: It doesn't keep me snug and warm if we're cuddled up naked. It's cold and slippery, and I prefer a toasty nest of arm or chest hair to sink my nostrils and cheeks into. It's primal and instinctual on my end to want to nosedive into a soapy smelling den of light brown or blond hairy love. I don't meld with dark Italian hair. The Italian pheromones don't match up for me.

Smooth skin: Where does the sweat soak into if the guy has no hair on his body? It doesn't. It slides and hangs around, and I'd likely have enough for both of us. A little bit of hair goes a long way in giving the beads of perspiration somewhere to dissolve.

Max was the first super tall, super smooth guy I dated the summer of 1997 when I interned for a local radio station, driving their company Jeep around, promoting sunscreen and their radio call number on the Jersey Shore. I was a communications major at Rider, unsure of whether I wanted to pursue journalism or a more public relations route, so I found something that fed my appetite for popular culture and communication. A radio station seemed like the best fit and living on the Jersey Shore carried with it a rapid summer pulse. I can't remember if my college found this opportunity or if I knocked on the door of the radio station's front door and inquired. The second one sounds more like me.

The first day of my internship I arrived at the downtown radio station office and met all the sales executives and radio talent. Max was in the mix and could not be missed. The electric between us was immediate and very distracting. *Shit. I can't go anywhere without falling into a thirst trap.*

We began dating within two weeks of my internship. It started with him flirting with me, me flirting back as I drove that white radio station-owned Jeep to participating bars and Shop Rites all over the Jersey Shore. "Are you hungry?" He asked after the first big event in Belmar's Shop Rite parking lot after I spent hours handing out travel sized sunscreen and the radio station Frisbees. "Yes. I am hungry." Over pizza and sodas, we got to know each other. Next came French kissing across his many tattoos and piercings when he wasn't wearing his suit for work. He lived with one of the owners of the radio station in a very comfortable house in my town. We had plenty of privacy for sex. Safe sex. I learned he had a five-year-old kid. But mostly I learned that he was hairless and very into always smelling clean. It made me overly self-conscious, but I was up for the challenge. His face was super smooth, and the lack of hair on his body a bit alarming. As we dated and the weeks unfolded, I figured out quickly that he was extremely narcissistic. And this became a strange piece of who we were as a couple. Our texture was chlorine and salt. Sort of sterile and only for two summer months. It's like the chemistry was of a cooler nature rather than fire. Fizzling, dying in seasonal change. He loved himself more than anyone—out of need, not vanity. What is it about young people that really want things to click together even when they aren't naturally doing that click-clack-stick. Is it our endless energy to win? To fuck? To be the one who changes the other's mind? The Savior Syndrome? The "I'm different than the others" disorder?

Brett came into my life around the time I got my very first job in publishing in Princeton circa 1999. We had gone to high school together but were sort of distanced by mutual friends and three years. He was the guy everyone loved to get along with in high school, and the guy with the brown station wagon everyone named *911*. He'd give anyone and everyone a lift as needed, and he spent his entire summers rescuing people on the beach as a lifeguard. His body showed that. Lean, muscular, and very strong. Like Max's, but Brett had a face you could trust. And hair on his body. I remember Brett's teeth and his clean breath. Always clean breath and very feathery brown hair like every 1980s sitcom crush. Remember Danny Amatullo from the 1982 series *Fame*? Lord help me, the feathered hair. Sigh.

It was the year 2000 and I somehow find myself in the arms of someone I had dated in 1998. For those of you who read my first memoir, it was Chip Ivy. I went back for a second try. Chip and I had a chemistry that worked. He always smelled so good, even when he shouldn't have. I can't remember if it was him or me who reached out. This was the guy I dated my third year at Rider University, while he attended Princeton. We had a fiery relationship that ended with his gift of a vibrator on my birthday. I was devastated, but after two years, I was over the disappointment and had gained new perspective and confidence upon graduating college. This time, I'd break his heart, but I didn't plan it that way. This time I had *him* wrapped around *my* finger, and again, unplanned.

For September of 2000 we dated again—in and out of his campus scene and around my new professional schedule while working for a business publishing house called TMC. I also sang in the beloved Dr. Doz Band at that time in my life—a Mercer County cover band, singing all the classic rock hits of the 1960s, '70s, '80s, and '90s. Life was good for a twenty-three-year-old. Our chemicals still exploded when we kissed, and there was nothing shabby about his smell or his sex. He wasn't smooth, nor overly hairy either. I knew deep down the physical part and the intellectual part were the two threads keeping us a couple. It was always the emotional thread missing with him, but since I was feeling super on top of my game, it didn't matter. I broke up with him for my first husband—a guy I went to college with, but barely interacted with while at Rider. He was more emotionally charged, and he said all the right things. I ended it with Chip Ivy. He was very angry. The last words he said to me were, "Don't ever even think of me again. Forget my name. Forget all of it." I did forget him. Except for his intelligence and that smell.

I suppose our olfactory truly knows the way to paradise, and we should pay attention like wolves and most other species when it comes to skin and sweat and everything that makes up the potential mates of our lives. No matter the boys and the arm hair and the past chapters of my life, I suppose the smells we stick with are the ones that we cannot get tired of in our older years—the smell of my dog's breath, the smell behind my husband's ear, the promise of a snowstorm, and a chocolate peanut butter explosion of any kind.

Being Skinny is Sensory

(CW: body dysmorphia)

The feeling of empty can be empowering. Empty leads to skinny, and then this is where we crash and burn. Or if we're one of the lucky ones, we figure out how to clear the destruction zone and see it in our rearview. Either way, we always carry with us the wreckage. It can lead to the most serious disorders, and it's not something to take lightly.

How I found skinny: it takes one person. Beth changed my trajectory. She was chic, sleek, hot as hell, and carried herself in a '90s goddess gait that spoke to me—you know the way: the *maybe-I'll-eat something-for dinner-maybe-I-won't-but-I-will-never-be-fat* way. When our mutual friend pledged a sorority at Rider University, Beth and I became close because why not. I watched her habits, emulated them, and lost a lot of weight without totally starving myself. I also had the metabolism of an athletic eighteen-year-old. We'd go to the gym, eat like birds, and wear bell-bottom jeans together. It was a sensation, inside-out. At night when I'd really feel the hunger that had built up all day from having a small bowl of cereal for lunch, I'd follow her lead by doing more sit ups and eating Mike and Ikes. It wasn't bread. It wasn't pasta. A highly active teenager can burn those delicious suckers off in minutes.

I was able to keep afloat with this weight loss and size loss for almost nine full months. Visiting home on weekends here and there made this challenging, but not impossible. My parents had a treadmill in the house, so there was that … it was the bread that killed the empty. The luscious Italian bread. I could cheat for two days straight and get right back on the skinny horse that Monday without seeing any weight gain. Like the bread never happened.

There are a few things that accompanied my skinny sensory state. One was a heightened horniness. When my body felt longer and leaner, I became enamored with my abdomen. I became entranced by the seduction I was capable of. I became aware of how attractive I might seem to the opposite sex, therefore why wouldn't I flaunt it with the newfound confidence that came with my smaller waist? Why wouldn't I walk past the wrestlers table in the dining hall a little bit slower than I had my first September in school? Why wouldn't I take the detour past the swimmers huddled near the outdoor gazebo in between classes, now that my stride was more correct within?

Once down to a skinny drumbeat, my musical tastes flickered around heavier alternative rock because with a waist that was this small, army boots and tight jeans, that's what the heavens want. Bush, Pearl Jam, and anything like it became my new old BFFs. I was not only as thin as Beth, but now a belly-chain wearing, aloof girl who didn't give it all away up-front girl. I loved it. We didn't wear all tight clothes. If something on us was form-fitting, the rest was baggy. You couldn't have it all form-fitting because that was what was known as "guido" in New Jersey. We were alternative, femme, and dirty-clean fierce.

°

I found myself attracted to a specific guy. Out-of-my-usual taste was a swimmer named Gregg, but everyone who knew him called him *Egg*. Is this someone I might've given a second glance before my newfound hotness? I don't think so—I matched his sort of athleticism now. Like, if he wanted to go for a run, I was confident I could keep up with him no problem. Or if he saw me naked, he wouldn't think—oh she's kind of curvaceous, and I can see she likes her bread, pancakes, and ice cream on the weekends. No—he'd say, jeez, look at her six pack. My newfound hotness alerted my already-friends too—"Why so thin?" Or "Don't go overboard." That attention gets very addictive, and frankly, it's a terrible thing. It's power, and it's a rush. That skinny empty is a concrete feeling in the bones and the veins and gives a girl new experiences that chubby girls don't have. Again, I know now how unhealthy and horrible this reality sounds.

How is being skinny a sensory experience exactly? For me, it conjured up feelings of extreme desire, ambition, and fireworks within. Looking back, I can pinpoint situations where it sort of, but didn't really, pay to be so empty:

— Driving to New Hope, Pennsylvania, an artsy community in Bucks County with my boyfriend at age nineteen. We were both broke and thirsty for adventure, so we took our low budget and his car down the country roads. I only saw him once a week, so I was also thirsty for his attention, and my flat stomach in my size six jeans felt like heaven. He noticed, he reacted, and we drank in the sunshine and trees.

— Home on holiday breaks, and for reasons I cannot recall, our family treadmill was in the dining room, with an outdoor view. I'd pop Tori Amos' *Boys for Pele* into my ears and run for the entire album. A plate of six saltines and a slice of American cheese waited as my reward. Clothes draped on me like I was a hanger, for the first time in my life. I felt unstoppable and very hungry.

— I attended a barbecue in the summer between college years, reuniting with some old high school friends. They saw how I had lost my freshman fifteen, rather than gained. I was hot. Period. I was the girl people sang about in 1990s rock alternative, and I didn't want to leave. I knew deep down it was all temporary, so I savored and swayed.

None of this was a growth mindset. None of this was the way to be. Yes, I was in great shape, which was the good part. But the skinny emptiness does not, by any means, equal happiness. Some people were potheads in college. Some were alcoholics. I was a hot girl. Which meant, in turn, I knew nothing.

Fat Flakes

I recently read a feature article about a restaurant in New Jersey where their signature dish was described as having a blizzard of parmesan shavings. That description rang so vibrant for me—so universal too, like we could put many categories of our life into this idea of a blizzard of shavings. At first, the obvious things we think about are pencil shavings, ice shavings—I've seen it used on menus to describe coconuts, chocolate, and mango on desserts. It always denotes a gourmet status, and it works when trying to get me to order the dish. It feels special.

In my mid-forties, I feel like I've endured a blizzard of friendship shavings. Remnants of friendships—hanging onto my heart like popcorn in molars and peach strings on the pit. Friends used to be my heart—blood sisters pumping through my strong Sicilian arteries, but now I'm a blizzard of sloppy crumbs. Traces of dirt all through the house. I forget how to be a friend in the way I was with them. Or maybe it's that losing that sisterhood caused the loss of skill. Fear replaces something deep within you when you are heart broken by friends who were supposed to be there for eternity. And when it's truly no one person's fault, but life's twists and turns to blame, it makes it even harder to brush those friendship shavings away.

All I want now is my comfortable navy-blue bathrobe and my friends in my books or on the screen. Streaming. Isn't that kind of sad? Blizzard of sad, and it smells like shower soap.

Yes, I made new friends and reconnected with old friends, but to get them to stick, and stay jaunty about our plans, dreams, goals, feels impossible some days. It turns out I am super drawn to individuals who prefer a tiny social circle, if any. We meet for lunch occasionally, we text, but the element of spontaneity on a summer night doesn't click for them. To be honest, I'm not a master of the last-minute structure either. Working hard at friendships is not natural for me anymore. I did it for so long and with so much energy that I'm plumb tired, as Amelia Bedelia would say. A blizzard of boredom some days. Unless I'm creating and writing or reading. During a snow blizzard, eating an arugula blizzard. Then a blizzard of toast. To cover up my blizzard of sad.

Back to the friendship shavings: I see my original sisters in photos, objects, I hear them in songs, and I can't cry. It does not make me weep, which in turn makes me more curious. I love new chapters in every aspect, but a blizzard of new requires diligence. New people, new quirks, new complaints, new dreams. It's all so exhausting. Blizzards and blizzards of tough things that sound like "Oh my gosh, you're so sweet. Thank you." "How are you today? Hope you're well." Just get to the real, plow through the pleasantries already. *I hear myself, yep.* I know a lot of this issue is embedded in my own crap. I am impatient, and I can be too intense too fast. Thank Goddess for my friend Bea who I've grown to love. I never see her for geographical and scheduling reasons, but I can be a hot mess with her over phone signals.

Bea and I met late in college because of an entanglement with my brother—they dated, and she and I clicked from the start. Time and life separated us for a while, but not completely.

And then once we both met our husbands, got married, had kids, our bond strengthened. Again, geography doesn't always allow us to be together in person, but she's always there for me, emotionally.

Some evenings my spirit feels like those green Romaine lettuce shreds when they're spread out like feathers. Still green and alive, but not in their organic form like a huge bird wing. Crunchy, fresh, and full of texture with the potential to wilt if I'm left too long in the cold or near the water. Who left me? My old friends. In a blizzard of 2020 anger on my part.

I was so very angry about injustice in the world, and all the things that wrap around those words—systemic racism, corrupt cops, lies, fake news, patriarchal bullshit—and that anger drove my sisters away. It made them very anxious. I don't fault them for it. It's not what they needed then. I took up way too much space with it, I suppose. One of them (because we are cordial and there's no hate shavings anywhere in this) remarked that one day we will meet for the first time again. When everyone involved is ready to sit at a table with bread and olive oil dip and not feel on edge, we will meet again for the first time. I am okay with this, and though I have doubts, the day will come.

My inner blizzard is visible to the naked eye when the wind blows a certain way. Therapy for four years has quelled the panic part, so now I have a more balanced blizzard that includes a smile, passion, with just a touch of insomnia some weeks. Oh, the most talented artist could illustrate this. Imagine a person and their blizzard components shooting out of the top of their skull and gusts of wind and shavings, colors, and shadows of all kinds.

In my present stage of life (let's call it the autumn of my life), the blizzard that feels most pressing is the spiritual one. Asking myself what I like, what feels good inside, what makes me happy, and how can I be peaceful but also ambitious toward my dreams. It's an inner blizzard that shakes and sweeps across hills and snow-covered gardens in my subconscious. It's a blizzard that welcomes my music, my tarot deck, my Palo Santo wood sticks, and my primordial sound mantra. It's a blizzard that's here to stay until the winter of my life, then who knows what blizzard awaits me there.

Charlie

Jenny Slate, in her memoir *Little Weirds* asks us to greet a person's dog prior to greeting the person. She claims it shows the kind of person you are. Six years ago, I had zero idea about this sentiment. Things have changed for me. I have the love of a dog, and it's something you only know if you live it. I can't imagine my life, my side, my couch, my chair, my kitchen, my yard, without our dog, Charlie. I see his soul in his eyes. I hear his love in his dog sigh. His undying loyalty to be where I am. As I write this, I feel his warmth nestled up on my leg. I greet people's dogs first.

My dog's breath, prior to his seventeen-teeth removal, could best be summed up as the Atlantic Ocean at low tide during a July evening when the sun is preparing to set. The scent rises into the beach air, ripe with dead clams, dead mussels, seaweed, salt, and brine. It's the time of day when all those scents mix up and wash over our nostrils like a lingering fart. Charlie is a rescue from Puerto Rico, post-Hurricane Maria. He originally was sent to my mom's best friend's mother, where he was loved so much. Unfortunately, his mom's eyesight was failing, so Charlie needed a better situation. He needed a fenced-in yard and someone to walk him daily. That's me. That's us.

We love Charlie very much—as much as all dog lovers love their dogs to immeasurable heights. We see his spirit, hear his goofy voice, and have learned to tolerate and actually miss his stinky breath when we're away on vacation. He's the best dog a family could wish for. There's one exception: he's an asshole around other dogs, but I suspect it's just him being only thirteen pounds and scared or hopeful. He's sleepy, playful, well trained, and he loves to be loved, particularly by my father. At part Phalene Papillon and part long-haired Chihuahua, he's truly an intelligent snuggle bug with a zoomie side to him post-poop.

Not having grown up with any dogs in my Mulberry Place home, I didn't anticipate the love. Having Charlie in my life has shown me what the real fuss about dogs is. It's about a deep, caring soul, capable of giving and receiving love that knows no limits. My family and I love him more than we can express, again, like most dog lovers. Charlie got us through the darker, uncertain days of the 2020 COVID-19 isolation periods. He's currently my shadow, my co-author, my Snoopy, and my little friendship-buddy man.

I do believe a dog would've mitigated some of my sensory things as a child, but in the same breath, I also believe that life events unfold as they're meant to unfold, with our nudges and pushes happening at simply the time they're supposed to happen. Charlie arrived in our lives in July 2019. My husband was the *most* hesitant, having cared for many dogs in his life. He had legitimate concerns about how a dog would affect our lifestyle, so we agreed on taking Charlie for a two-week trial period. After forty-eight hours, Kevin looked at me, his face nuzzled in Charlie's scruff and said, "I love him." Kevin loves dogs very much, and they love him.

When a dog pushes up against your back or your side as you're sleeping or approaching sleep, this is a sign of love. They nudge and slide into their space that belongs to them, as close to you as possible. Charlie likes to do this with me in two different ways. One is when I am writing on my keyboard and he nestles tightly to my side. Maybe he will sleep, or maybe he wants to clean his paws. To feel Charlie's breathing, his warmth, and to watch how he looks for the steps in our daily routines and rituals. There is nothing purer and more instinctual on Earth than a dog's love for their humans.

The second way Charlie confirms his love for me is the night-time squish against my side. I'm a left side sleeper, so he enjoys pushing his backside against the right side of my body. As close as he can get. And we both exhale. It's a good thing Kevin and I are not snugglers!

I Said It Out Loud

I had the procedure completed in my mind. I prepare, mourn, and process thunderous events before they occur. By doing it this way, I can move forward faster, knowing I buried the bruise, so that when it happens, if there are any surprises, I have room for them in my brain. It works ninety-seven percent of the time. I know I'm lying to myself to minimize the fear. I still do it. I do it because who else will protect me better than I will protect me?

My MRI-guided needle biopsy fell in the three percent of the times that processing trauma ahead of time didn't work. A week before the procedure, I sat in my green recliner at home, legs up, hands on my chest and let my breath settle and rise. I'd learned it from my Reiki Master—the art of breath and how it works to clear the noise in our headspace. The point of the biopsy needle would be tiny, the puncture crisp, but I wouldn't feel it. It aimed for the lump hidden behind all of the things that make breasts plump. I envisioned braids—glands, veins, and muscle, twisted around one another with eyes of goblins and dragons. Not necessarily evil. Simply ... aggressive. Those evil specks and blobs would witness this sterile silver instrument headed straight for their heart—a disruption to their mandala of complex design. It would kill their routine. Knowing at any moment they might lose and maybe I wouldn't have cancer. I'd have a glorious Bjork song in my head for comfort during the procedure because music always soothes me in tough situations. I was prepped. I opened my eyes and made myself lunch, pretending to forget about the looming procedure day.

The day always arrives, doesn't it? My blue and white floral hospital gown flowed before me, untied in the front, of course. A human being tends to sit up super straight in these clinical situations. "Relax," the soft spoken technician urged as she smeared alcohol on the side of my left breast and part of my armpit. The mass in question was deep, close to my nipple, and unable to be felt by a hand or finger on the outside. Many lumps hide like this, which is why you keep up with your yearly screenings. Breasts are beautiful, complicated, and nothing short of staunch creations that both represent life, and for too many women, death.

Dr. Lenora stood in front of me explaining the MRI-guided procedure in her gray pencil skirt, hands in her lab coat pockets. Her thick brown curls might indicate we were cousins if a stranger met us in a cafe. She was gentle and very thorough. I imagined our places switched and how that type of empathy was always important to remember when she spoke to her patients. I imagined her interacting with her family at a holiday table, talking about her patients of all ages and how "breast cancer was a disease that needed a cure yesterday." She'd reach for an olive as her bangle bracelets jingled over the plate. Her nails short, manicured and painted in a friendly grayish-blue.

"We do see a lot of progress though. But not enough," she'd add before sipping her red wine.

I heard what she was saying, and what my writer-brain designed for her—that holiday table with a giant antipasto and a bottle of sparkling water in front of her and her three sisters. In the middle of the table were oranges stabbed with cloves—to ward off evil spirits. Her mom at the other head of the table talking about how she wished their father were alive to see his girls and all they've accomplished. She'd peel a pear with her arthritic hands and the same knife she'd be using for decades. "We don't have breast cancer in our family," her mom uttered.

"It doesn't matter, Ma."

I cleared my throat and wanted to ask so many more questions, but my voice felt small. She read my mind instead.

"It shouldn't hurt at all. Maybe minimal pressure but tell us if you're uncomfortable."

That's what Dr. Lenora said to me in front of everyone in our white-walled radius in the radiology department of my local hospital. Who knew that I'd be in the small percentage of women whose breasts wouldn't welcome the lidocaine? The aggressive creatures inside my breasts decided they'd make my life harder, after all. I had known in my early twenties that this would happen, I swear. I knew I'd get breast cancer, but all I had to do was wait until forty-two years old. It was a hunch that originated during my obsession with the statistics.

"So once you're in the MRI machine you cannot move an inch. It will affect the images. I know it will be hard to remain totally still, but it's critical that you do."

"How long will it last in that machine? I know I'll be face down, but still," I asked. Times and boundaries always comfort me.

"It shouldn't take more than thirty minutes, as long as we get the needle in sturdy and precise," she said, birthday cake in her tone.

"And this won't hurt?" I asked, despite her answering the question earlier. Everyone does it.

"It shouldn't, no. The numbing agent does its job well," she said. I'm certain she wanted to rip up those words an hour later. Like a crappy first draft full of excessive em dashes. I'm sure she wanted to hug me that day, but professionals know better.

Essentially, these MRI-guided biopsy results would determine how it's going to be for the next year of my life. Would I be radical, or would I live year-to-year with a calm mindset toward my breast health? A needle in my breast, then through the MRI machine because so far, women's health technology lags behind. To truly pinpoint the mass, I've been through at least four other types of screenings.

Breasts are woven like webs and caverns and knitted masterpieces, but also more women need to be in positions of power for us to access better healthcare. My hospital, closest to where my children attend school and our home, didn't have access to the most advanced technology. I was on a time crunch to get this procedure completed, so I couldn't drive farther north. It had to be part of my regular day. That being factual, it's likely my experience would've gone the same way anywhere. Even the advanced technology isn't one-stop shopping.

"Steph is prepping the area where the needle will insert, but in a moment I will guide the needle into the breast, and then based on the images while inside the MRI machine, I will take as much tissue sample as we can grab on and near the mass." She paused. I chewed my thumbnail as far as it would go when she looked away. She rested her hand on my shoulder.

The hot, stinging deepness of silver. Bjork was out of earshot. "You'll be great."

While administering the lidocaine needle, which was much smaller than the biopsy needle, Dr. Lenora remained focused and quiet. I appreciated her grace. A chatty medical professional is fine in some instances, but not this one. Her demeanor was steady, hand warm in the glove. I trusted her. I believed in trusting my physicians.

"Just a pinch for the lidocaine to settle in and numb the area," she whispered, but louder. "There. Let's wait a second." Seconds feel like rusty nails, but I tried so hard to imagine diamonds.

I exhaled. Bjork song. Bjork song.

"I'm not keeping my breasts if it's cancer. Even if it's tiny." I don't mean to say it out loud. Can't scoop the words back into your mouth like you can a spoonful of sprinkles that never touched the ice cream. I made my decision. Out loud.

"I agree. Breasts like to make trouble. And just because we think it's stage two, often it's higher once we get in there. Getting a bilateral mastectomy is a smart move." I hadn't expected that. I was soaring above the table, and I was terrified. She agreed, which meant this was serious.

My mind returned to her mom's holiday table, her sisters nodding along as they scooped salami and peppers onto their porcelain plates painted with Kate Spade precision. Mom's enjoying that orange, more relatives were piling in, and Johnny Mathis was blaring through the house.

MRI guided biopsies in the breast are one of the last steps in finding the exact location of the mass. The suspicious mass that will determine so much about your life as a mom, patient, wife. The mass they found weeks ago in a 3D mammogram involved pressing and smashing my double-Ds (once healthy Bs prior to children) between two cold metal plates for thirty minutes. Despite the lovely technicians' efforts to make my experience as comfortable as possible, my breasts were flung and smashed. With a look in the technician's eyes that say, I know women's health technology isn't where it should be, but I will make up for that with my soft touch, I promise.

"Okay, now for the biopsy needle. You can lie on your stomach with your head through the hole where you see the mirror. This is how you will lay once in the machine," she said I saw her mom again, winking at her from across the antipasto as her sisters notice. She was Dad's favorite, making women's lives better every day. Angela Lenora.

Then the biopsy needle.

I remembered my green recliner meditation breath cycle. It wasn't helping.

The pressure of a thousand tweezers pressed into my breast. The stars they talk about, but they aren't stars you see. They're of a colder breed. My left side was in flames. My spirit, steamrolled, like black snow full of gravel.

"OUCH. I can feel it. I can feel it. I can feel—" I said and swallowed my oncoming sob.

"She's bleeding so much! Look!" A technician behind me yelled. My spirit, ice cold.

"It's okay. She's okay. You're okay," Dr. Lenora said, surely giving that technician a motion of her head to calm the hell down. "You're okay." She stroked my head, while yet another technician held my hand. Her nails tickled my scalp. My left side, on fire. Help me.

"It ... hurts ... so ... much ..."

I saw my grandmother now, sitting on her yellow stepstool in her apartment kitchen below her landline telephone on the wall. Arms folded over her maroon cardigan, with a giant smile, watching me eat her veal over polenta. That narrow kitchen that smelled like garlic and lilacs fighting.

I felt the needle. I felt it. Gram left and all I could see in front of me were old white men making up these procedures knowing they'd never need them done on their bodies. Barbaric and repeated and unclear because breasts are as complex as women. It required too much work and budget to result in something tidy and comfortable. Yet every breast surgeon is magnificent. They feel bad that some of the technology falls flat.

"I am so sorry. The numbing agent is not working on you." She was still stroking my head so lightly. "But I need you to be strong and let us continue. We need these images."

"There's ... There's no other cream or numbing agent you can—" I squeaked, head down in the head-hole. "Please?" I felt the technician wiping up the blood oozing out of the hole the needle made in my breast. On the ground, on the MRI machine.

"There isn't. You can do this. You can."

"Okay," I say. "Roll me into the machine. NOW."

"We just have to push this breast with the needle in this hole to get the images."

More movement. More pain. More pressure. I was out near Neptune's orbit. Gone.

With heavy metal buzzing in my ear, a thick needle sticking halfway in and halfway out of my breast, they obtained the images. I left my body for a while while I was in that machine. I thought about that veal over polenta and my grandmother's hand in mine. Her dangling rosary on her bed frame. The photo of my mom with her beehive hair in 1966 on Gram's dresser. Gram's hands were cold hands, but better to keep me from vomiting while in the machine. Her Italian accent sung over the metal buzzing of the MRI.

"Quin-DE-SEE-Bella. Oh, how I loved the day you were born." The metal clangs muted. The needle dulled. The din of my nerves lightened. I found my breath. Sank into Gram's shoulder. She dipped her cookie in her coffee. Next to the bowl of quartered lemons for the veal.

"I don't want to die, Grandma." Now I knew there was cancer. I just knew it.

"You won't," she said.

It ended. I couldn't stop trembling on my lonely walk out of the building to find my ride home. My dad. But I couldn't let him see my pain or my tears. I'd save it for myself when I replayed this over and over in my mind a couple of years later. I'd save it for when I had brand new breasts made from my belly fat, knowing I'd never need a mammogram ever again. I opened the car door like so many women before me. "Hi."

"How'd it go?"

"Fine."

Like so many women before me.

Oh My Donna

When my oldest child turned about two years old, I had been out of the public-school classroom for two years. I kept a few private reading students on a tutoring basis, but for the most part, I was a mom all day. We'd easily flood our mornings and afternoons with outdoor excursions, playdates, and visits with my husband's stepmom, Grandma Juli. We'd do Shop Rite runs, playground tours, and all kinds of mommy-and-me classes. I'd read aloud, nonstop. Then it happened. I got extremely creative-restless and my anxiety increased a few notches because of it. I wasn't creating anything, and my body knew it, so it reacted. I also happened to throw my lower back, in the lumbar region, very out of whack. I am a really devoted power-walker (sometimes I push it into a jog), but my friend at the time had invited me to an old school Jazzercise class to switch things up. My back was like ... nope. I also hadn't discovered the proper sneaker brand for my kind of arch and stride, so that too, contributed to the muscle mess. My lower back was out.

Here I am with a two-year-old, back out, miserable, restless, anxious, and frustrated because I like to move. Since it was a priority for me to be social all the time for the sake of my child, I invited my friend Stephanie and her daughter, Akiana, over for a playdate. Steph saw my pain. She had massive intuition, being a lifelong yogi.

"What is going on with that limp?" she asked me.

"I threw my back out."

"Yikes."

For an hour or two we ate the eggplant pasta I had made a few nights before and watched the kids play and tumble on the back deck made of gray composite. When the girls fell down it didn't hurt the way wood did. She must've been exhausted from watching me lumber and limp all over the place, so she asked me to put myself in child's pose.

Stephanie placed her palms in the lower muscles of my back while I remained in child's pose and she kept her eye on the little ones.

"Hmm," she said, with her toasty, Sanskrit-sweet smile. "Yeah."

She held her hands there, and I felt a sensation that can only be described as a glimmer of sunlight. It felt like a jolt, but a soft one, and it's not like I stood straight up and was cured. But I felt the muscles in my lumbar region open up a bit, and the next day when I woke up I was sixty percent better.

She told me it was called Reiki. In the weeks that followed, I read up on it and found a local Reiki therapist named Donna Keeney. Donna Keeney's presence in my life changed me and my sensory issues forever. She has affected hundreds of people's lives having trained under very intense instructors in various fields of energy work, one of them being Deepak Chopra.

Though I can't remember who lead me to Donna, she came highly recommended for everything Reiki. I attended a few of her sessions prior to becoming attuned in Reiki I—shares, info sessions, anything she hosted through a local yoga center.

There are three levels of Reiki certification, and then a Master level which I have never felt drawn too. I'm three levels certified all with Donna and *only* Donna.

Reiki means universal energy. It's a gentle practice that works similar to the way acupressure needles do, except there's no needles. Only hands, Japanese symbology, breathing, and a sprinkle of faith in what's happening. The Reiki therapist is not a healer. Stop that. The recipient's body is doing the work with the help of the Reiki symbology and the hands. I learned white light Reiki from Donna, and it's hands-on. Hands above is silly. Sorry. Put the hands on the body.

My first level of training—I remember every detail about that six-hour day. I trained with two other people in a small space that Donna rented in a very old building in downtown Toms River on Main Street. It was an old two-story home, likely built in the early 1700s. It smelled like old books and the floors were wooden and crooked, the hallways narrow. Donna's rented space was on the second floor in a room the size of a small bedroom. The other two Reiki trainees and I sat on a couch facing Donna who sat on her stool. There were very interesting pictures of humans on the wall behind her. One of them was a woman's face in black and white charcoal except for her piercing blue eyes. It was clearly a mystic or a woman who knew things, whether she was real or fictional, I never asked. The thing that got me though, and made me feel at home and like I was genuinely supposed to be there, was the green lamp on her desk. We had the same one in my house and in my bedroom for a while. Then my brother had it in his. Eventually it landed in my dad's garage. There was something about its presence that made me feel in good hands. Like I trusted Donna right away, as silly as it sounds—a lamp as an artifact of trust, but I felt it.

She guided us through a meditation. We were going to meet our very first spirit guide. Spirit guides are your resources when your intuitions open wide and long and deep. When your soul and spirit aren't afraid to see more than what's here on Earth. It's the best way I can describe it. I remember one of the people training with me had very Native American spirit guides. Visions of ancestry, land, and tribe. Donna had us share afterward if we wished. My spirit guide, whom I still but rarely call upon when I practice, is a young child named Holly in the snow with very rosy cheeks and a pink snowsuit on. I can still see the snow-covered yard I saw her in. She was happily playing. There was a wired fence like the one in my yard on Mulberry, and the air was silent. The point of spirit guides is to remind you the other side is real. They give you permission to let go of fear and hesitance. Holly met me and never said a word. She's my inner snow child, and though I never have to ask for her or conjure her up, I know she lingers in my subconscious when I practice any energy or tarot work.

As the Reiki training progressed, Donna explained the three main symbols and their use. We meditated some more, shared some more, and then broke for lunch. It wasn't until after lunch that I experienced what I will never forget until the day I die. Donna using her own Reiki on me for the first time. Even though my friend Stephanie had placed her hands on my lumbar spine while I was rolled up in child's pose and I felt the stars shooting out of her fingertips, I had never experienced Reiki from someone as seasoned and connected as Donna. This was her lifeblood, her bread and butter, and how she earned a living. This is what she did every day for many years, often side by side with physicians. In addition, Donna was not working on my back. Unlike Steph, she was working in my solar plexus area and up by my heart chakra.

I don't think she had her hands on me for more than two full minutes before I started freaking out. The electricity and fear that shot through me was intense and unexpected. At the time, and not until Donna explained what was happening to me, I thought it was fear. It *was* fear *and* everything else; it was me reacting openly and honestly to the Reiki. I was allowing it in, and it was sinking in, and unblocking stuff. It was joggling around whatever needed to burst out. I shook; I panicked; all while Donna breathed calmly. She said very matter-of-fact (she's not the fluttering butterfly you would think when you think of an energy worker, she is the opposite—serious, poker-faced, and focused as hell), "Elaina, let it happen. Trust it." I wanted to jump off the table and out the window onto the lawn and run home, and she knew it. "Elaina. You're safe. You're okay." I continued to squirm under her touch, but I forced myself to breath at her pace.

Eventually the panic ceased, and I finally calmed down. I still felt the nodes and beams and energy from her hands in a way I never have since, but I breathed. Then I cried. She said I might also cry the next day, and the name of this condition is known as a healing crisis. It happens when we release things that needed to be gone. Or when something very blocked gets unblocked. It can be a physical pain, emotional pain, and everything in between and wrapped up as combinations, kind of like smoothies or Playa Bowl goodies. Our bodies know. The Reiki gives the body a sort of permission to just fucking let it go. It's kind of beautiful.

After I experienced Reiki from Donna, we practiced on each other—identifying and verbalizing what we felt or envisioned or knew. The energy. The information. The sensation. Donna officially attuned us and opened us up with her own brief meditation and a few waves of her wand. Just kidding. No wands. This attunement might have been prior to our practice session, now that I think of it.

For two months afterward, I practiced on friends for free. They'd come to my house on my newly purchased massage table, or I'd go to their place. It was fascinating and exhausting, and I loved it all. I'd relay the information I got during sessions. For me, names became a thing. Often, they were family that had passed. Sometimes they were town names relevant to their lives. Sometimes I'd see animals. Then we'd look up the symbology for each. I'd pick up on physical ailments, and a few times the person on my table would cry uncontrollably because that's what they needed that day and their body knew it. When that happened, I reacted the way Donna had to my anxiety. I told them they were safe, that they were okay, and to let it out.

By the two-month mark I was ready for level II. Some people go to the next level after a week, some a year, some never. This training was me alone with Donna in the same old house. Reiki II is about absentee Reiki, so it's chock full of symbols and words that correspond to the symbols. Donna opened the second training the same way as the first level—with a deep guided meditation to discover a second spirit guide. There, I encountered a peacock. I talked about this meditation—this one strayed from my beloved winter snow and more into a sunset in June kind of vibe, with a large, gorgeous peacock to greet me. The name Cecelia was present but wasn't the name of the bird. The rest of the day I learned the most important strand of Japanese symbols involved in providing Reiki for someone who is not present. I have used this strand more times than I can count in my life. When you work with this set of symbols, you work in a dark, quiet space and you focus and receive the information for the recipient. I always tell the person I'm working on everything, even if it feels bizarre to tell them that you see a peach sweater on the chair in the room. Yep. Reiki II training was much less intense by nature—at this point I was close friends with Reiki itself. Donna and I walked a mile or so to have lunch. It was a sunny day, and we both seemed content. It was the level of Reiki training that remains my favorite and could be why I really love practicing Reiki II when I have the time and silence to do it for people who ask.

Reiki III training didn't call to me as quickly. I practiced endlessly between levels two and three, almost as if I had to feel worthy of signing up for level three. That is not at all how it works, but for me personally, it's the headspace I had to been in to be at ease with myself and the practice. I allowed a full year and a half or more until I texted Donna to let her know I was finally prepared to become attuned in the third level. She invited me to her home on the river in Pine Beach. It's as beautiful as it sounds. Her late husband, Billy, had designed and built a unique home on the river years before his death—windows, wood, and refuge is what comes to mind. There were close six of us. We spread out in her very open and very inviting living room. It was an open floor plan, so really, we were simply spread out in the home. It didn't feel closed in, nor isolated from, the river view, just a room away. It all felt very Donna—the shoreline, summer, family.

Donna fed us nourishing food, introduced us to each other, and made the July afternoon feel like a true retreat. We chose our most comfortable spot in her high-ceilinged family room and admired the raw and natural woods in her riverfront home. The rustic decor and warmth of her home matched Donna's huge brown eyes and very curly hair. She is a very naturally beautiful woman and when you sit near her, you feel how special she is. She's not warm and fuzzy and overly friendly. She's charming, intelligent, and highly matter of fact.

She led us through our third level meditation. This time I didn't meet a spirit guide but instead a location. I found myself in the ceiling of my aunt Connie's gift shop looking down on years of hard work and abundance. No one else was there, but I felt the history of the store lingering up in those beams and shelves. The light was barely on. I wasn't afraid. I was sort of home. Donna said it was probably because it's where I felt Connie's love as a child.

The day unfolded with more intricate patterns than the first two trainings. Reiki III is more complex and required my full attention. More symbols, more concentration, more knowledge to receive, and a ton more practice. She had us complete an exercise where one of us sat in a chair in front of everyone else. She had us "scan" the chaired person for blockages and information. It was like nothing I had ever done or would think to do. But I did it, and I surprised myself. She pushed us past our meditative limits and got us to a place of real understanding of Reiki. I mean, as much as anyone can understand and interpret it after an eight-hour day of training.

The real understanding, like with any other practice, comes with work. Doing it. My head pounded in the last hours of the training from all the stimulus, sharing, and information. Offering and administering Reiki to people who seek it. I remember during our break it was a torrential downpour and thunderstorm. The sky became so dark, like it knew. It knew we were also seeking a breakthrough of sorts. My headache was relentless, but I needed to complete the training, and I did. When I returned home that July evening, I scrubbed myself with Epsom salt and collapsed in bed for a very long night's sleep.

o

For the decade that followed my three levels of training, I worked on many people. It was fulfilling work. Then when my second child was born I had nothing left to give anyone else in terms of energy. I started writing, and just like that, my new outlet was established. Reiki kind of took a backseat. But it never goes away, and it doesn't take a lot to reignite the flame.

So here I am with all these spectacular tools. And I have them at my disposal as I needed them for my family and close friends, at this point. When I have lunch with friends of the same seed and moon, the energies swirl above us, and the typical eavesdropper would have a lot to report on. "Yeah, these two women were sort of ... reading each other's minds?" It's never that clear-cut. But yeah, it's the gist. The company I love to keep usually dabble in the energy arts. I feel very lucky to understand and have this portion of my brain exercised.

Dear Neck,

Hello cervical spine, you demon crawler, midnight hellish man with your foolish language. I mean it though. You're the rotten apple in my body—you hang on to every god damn word and worry, and I'm over it. Like right now, as I am trying to have a meaningful and rich literary experience with peers in my online writing class, you're bent out of shape, twisted, crunchy, and making my head explode in pain. Above my right eye. But it always originates with you. Always. Then I resort to watching neck adjustments on Instagram, like Dr. Tubio in Houston who cradles his patients' head and neck in his meaty arms and shoulders, pulls, distracts, then pops the living daylights out of them and I long to feel that release. I long to feel Dr. Tubio stretch you out, bend you ever so gingerly, then jerk you in the direction that puts you back into your place.

Cervical spine, you're an asshole. Always lurking around the corner on long drives to Vermont, in closed spaces, in hot restaurants. It always begins and ends with you. It always pinches in your root, your stem, shoots up my head, down my shoulders. God damn, let it go once in a while. But usually you wait for Dr. Beck to manipulate your situation. So that I scream, "Whoa. *Oh my god,* did you hear that?" He put you in your place. Rearranged your notes, your utterings, your stubborn verbs, the way you make me clench up. Sometimes to the point of dry heaving because the pain you induce can be nauseating.

One day maybe you'll talk to the others and give them a chance to hold on tight. You're way too central in my life anymore.

Give up your kingdom. Give up your power. Give me some space.

Then give your follower bones the same.

Space.

To breathe.

Elaina

P.S. Do not forget your hormones are all over the place at this point in your life, and that is part of your knots. Your tension. Your "please crack my back."

Melting

If you don't get a text back from me within hours, there's a good chance I am one of three places—with my dog, reading on my green chair, watching Scandinavian detective/murder shows, or melting away in a massage chair in the mall at the very clean, very efficient Asian Therapy. The doors are open, and it's wide open and spread out. It's itchy living in suburban New Jersey—expensive, crowded, and salty. It requires a person to unwind every now and then. In those massage chairs, I become dough. Mush. Oatmeal. My body is simply a physical piece of flesh both connected and strangely disconnected to my soul in those twenty-five minutes in the chair massage chair.

The massage therapist sets the handheld portable white timer to twenty minutes. Five beeps total. I throw my coat, wallet and phone into the canvas bin behind the chair she points to, pointing to the designated chair I will melt into today. She grabs the single paper towel to place over the headrest where my hair line will be, framing my face.

"Can I have two paper towels, please? Is that okay?"

"Two?" she asks.

"Yes." She thinks I'm a total weirdo, like one more sheet of paper towel will protect me from any random germs living on that headrest. I take the gamble anyway and bet on the second paper towel.

My head faces the ground, her shoes, but soon my eyes will remain closed, and I will enter purple-splotches-behind-my-eyes town where the single most enjoyable version of heaven on Earth abounds.

It's so instant for me. Strong hands, fingers, knuckles reaching into the knots on my shoulders. The response is organic and all-consuming.

Is she thinking back to her training and philosophy or simply acting person to person, knot to knot? The double elbow press from cervical to lumbar in between the vertebrae. Integers. The systematic rhythm is part of the relief for me. It's an orchestra that my body approves of with an enormous stamp.

My world spins on a cycle of liquid bliss when I am in that chair. It all flows when the pressure of the fingers dig into me. Staccato fingertips or elongated elbow dredging through my tight muscle wiring.

College Fingers

My college years were really the beginning of my melting mission. I chased down decompression. I chased it the way my peers chased alcohol and drugs. I didn't want weed. I wanted someone to brush my hair. Or to crack my back. I chased it like a fiend. My friend Kim recently said to me when we had coffee, "Oh my god Laina, do you remember in Olsen (our dorm) you'd see me walk by your room and you'd yell out—KIM! Come brush my hair!" I have no recollection of this, but it makes me chuckle to no end, and I believe it.

You can't make up shit like that. I wanted my hair brushed, my scalp rubbed, and like I said, my back cracked. It wasn't a bone crack. It was that thing that happens to the built-up gas within the air sacs between the vertebrae, and once I discovered how it happened, my person was JC. And then I got him addicted to it too. "JC. Crack my back!" "Okay, darling. Lie down. Then it's my turn." And we'd take turns, face and stomach down on his dorm carpet and we'd start between the shoulders and slowly make our way down as the air sacs popped, and it felt like relief. The noise itself. I chased it. I chased the bodily decompression. I learned how to use corners of shelves, filing cabinets, really any structure I could jab into my shoulders.

Besides the hair brushing and the back cracking, I found out that my shoulders needed this kind of expedition too. My dear friend Bob had particularly strong hands. From playing guitar, rolling joints, and a dabble in drums. I'd position myself in criss-cross-applesauce on his dorm rug while he sat above me on his bed. I got a new dose of Xanadu. His fingers found my knots. His fingers found the anxiety crickets woven into my muscles. And with slow and instinctual digging, I was putty on his floor. My sky opened with every press and dig. And once he uttered the words, "We could never have sex if you think this feels good. You'd die." We laughed hard. Bob and I weren't like that, but I understood his point. A secret: I'd rather have my neck and shoulders dug into any day over sex. Easy. The activities are like apples and oranges, but I'd rather relax than climax.

Neck Movies

I'm not a chiropractor student, nor will I ever be. But watching the human reaction to his head hug and technique relaxes me. Watching the neck move into place makes me feel less pain, knowing I'll likely visit my chiropractor within a week of watching—it serves as a reminder. Humans react with so many emotions after their neck is adjusted. And everyone's neck moves differently depending on which cervical C1-C5 needs to be moved. Sometimes the occipital bone needs movement. The type determines the sound—some adjustments are ripply. Some are jolting cracks. Some sound like a zipper. Some sound like a bunch of rocks falling into place. It depends. And even the largest of men cry and laugh and sometimes both.

But why do I watch this, you ask? It's a study in humanity and sensory issues for me. Because for about ten years now, getting my neck adjusted is how I am shifted back into my best human form. When Dr. Beck moves my neck back to where it's supposed to sit, I am capable of an hour-long conversation without trying to crack my neck myself. Even though it might not require adjusting, I convince myself it will make my headache disappear. When the neck is adjusted, I'm capable of focusing on my writing. I'm a better mom and wife. My neck is where my daily stress sits. Where the conversations with my mom sit. The bullshit of toxic people in the world lives in my neck. The adjustments melt it all away. Watching the adjustment of the human neck makes me feel a certain vicarious relief. Is it weird? You bet. We all have our things.

On the Table

I want to talk about the table massage because I can undoubtedly frame and organize past events in my life based on massage therapy centers and their proximity and course of my lifestyle at the given time. My very first massage was when I was twenty-three years old and working in Princeton. Ten seconds into the massage my nose ran like a faucet, onto the floor below the table, as I was face down. The therapist said, "Oh no worries.

Here's a tissue. It's very common for first-timers. We're joggling things around that have never been jiggled before." Now, years later, I understand she meant my lymphatic system.

Following this first experience on a massage table were dozens of massages, all varying, depending on the style of the therapist. All slightly different with some similar patterns and styles, and all with their own level of skill and abundance in the realm of opening what's lost and blocked. I remember being in St. Lucia for my honeymoon in a covered outdoor space. That massage was tranquil and stretchy. The therapist clearly with a script and a style more vacation resort mode. I didn't mind at all.

Then there was my Las Vegas massage in a hotel chain where the spa was intimidating and brand-centric, and again, performed with a pattern. This very pricey massage was one of the least memorable, as the therapist practiced too much caution with the amount of pressure and held back on really working the knots. It was more of a scan and skim. Like eating a large bowl of plain, mediocre vanilla ice cream. It's still ice cream. But that's it.

Christy

Enter my mom's long time massage therapist, Christy. Christy was very special. She was the only person I'd let massage me during my pregnancies. She was calculated and creative and listened to my body. Christy was strong, graceful, and very in tune with the striations and muscles of our Italian architecture.

OG Massages

For a brief period in my life, I lived on the Route One corridor of New Jersey out by New Brunswick. My first husband and I had a townhouse in a town called North Brunswick—a highly populated, highly congested, highway-based part of central NJ. It was a drivable distance from my teaching job at St. Cecelia's in Iselin where I taught Pre-K. I managed to locate an Asian-owned massage center in the Edison part of Route One. It was a small space with about four massage tables and uniformed therapists. This was one of the best massage practices in my memory of my probably two hundred massages so far. The center was covered in reflexology charts, meridian charts, and sparkling clean in every corner. If I had to estimate, I probably stopped in twice a month for an hour massage on my way home from work when I wasn't carpooling with my friend Cathy. These massage practitioners were extremely strong, very assertive, and had a clue about what each human body needed individually. This is where one woman said to me, while I was half awake and about thirty minutes into my massage—"Your nails. You bite them because you're missing vitamins." At twenty-four years old I think she was correct. All I knew was I was melted into the table and far off in outer space. "Okay," I muttered, as she continued the knot undoing like the artist she was.

Years later when my current and permanent husband (until death parts us) and I lived in Bradley Beach, I had the massage surprise of my life. The tiny Asian woman in a small place I had found online asked me if she could walk on my back. Of course, I said yes. She hoisted herself up onto the massage table, grabbed the parallel bars secured into the ceiling above me, and danced across my back, using her toes like tools. She was able to pinpoint miniscule knots between the vertebrae. I highly recommend finding a practice to try this at least once. It's a fine art and requires training and true instinct.

There have been random times in my life when I gave the franchise massage center a shot, thinking, they must hire training professionals, right? Yes. But skill without style, instinct, and gift shows. And leaves you feeling empty and unsatisfied the way you feel after a book that let you down.

Friends Who Massage

My friend Danyele is the cure for those mediocre franchise experiences. Talk about gift and instinct. She tells me when I need a neck adjustment because she can feel the bones that are out of whack. She knows when things just aren't lined up. She knows where certain areas are "clogged." Most importantly, she is strong as a bull.

Malls

The mall near my house is crap for the most part. So many stores have closed, but even pre Covid, it just never felt like the experience it was in the earlier years with bustle and beat. It's lost its electricity, figuratively. The one positive thing left in my mall is the highly successful and highly friendly Asian Therapy massage place. It's been in a couple of locations in the mall since its arrival about fifteen years ago. It currently occupies the space that Payless once leased, so it's wide and spacious. Since I have known them, they pay attention to sanitizing protocols and the owner is very aware of his repeat customers. I've never had a negative experience here. I leave in a daze, in a rosy-cheeked fog, and very pliable. Mostly I request twenty-minute chair massages, but once in a while I ask for a forty-five-minute table massage behind the safe, wispy, opaque curtains.

You go behind the opaque curtain and remove all your clothing except for your underwear. This includes no bra because keeping one of those on is just ludicrous. Might as well be fully clothed if you're not going to remove it. You lay yourself face first on the table with your face in the hole. And then you cover your body with the clean white sheet they provide. Your massage therapist will shortly enter the area through the curtain door, but not before asking if you're ready. They lower the sheet and often tuck it into the rim of your underwear. Your entire back is their canvas.

I know how to detach right about now. I am a human, but merely a body of muscle, skin, and bones. And intertwining molecules and matter in between. They are the conduit in which my body will receive pressure where it calls for it. For the next forty-five minutes I see purple blotches behind my eyes. In Reiki that's what I see when the channels open wide and the body is allowing itself to heal. With the help of the conduit, in this case, the massage therapist. You sink into the motions. You allow the tightness to melt. You see the closest thing to your heaven on Earth. It's not for every-body, but I urge you to open yourself up to feeling this vulnerable and open. It shifts and moves things around that often require movement and shifts. Early in the massage the pressure level requires my consent—"Too hard? Harder?" This sets up how effective the remainder of the experience will proceed.

When a strong, yet cautious person who understands the skull structure in relation to the muscles and ligaments in its vicinity digs their fingers in, right at the base, I travel far away. Sometimes I travel directly to what can only be the bridge to heaven or the various homes and yards I've seen in my dreams. Maybe it's where I lived in 1885, in a small house in the country with a clothesline attached to my kitchen window, extending across to the mature oak tree on my lawn.

My habit of getting massage has grown into a self-care need, rather than a luxury, yet I still only get one every four to eight weeks. It does the trick for me. I think it's most important to listen to our bodies and what they want. Do they want to be stretched? Do they want to be woken up? Settled down? We're all twisted and manufactured uniquely, and so I can only share my experience as a person who requires pressure to feel less pressure.

The Benefits

As someone who is both enhanced and diminished by her nervous system which is directly responsible for the way I perceive temperature, smells, and touch, I think it's worth celebrating more than lamenting. To be able to live my life in waves and art. To create. I feel lucky. I don't think it would be possible without my sensory stuff. I really think it was meant to mold who I am for the rest of my life. Even if it meant nausea, headaches, and insomnia.

In his memoir *The Storyteller,* Dave Grohl refers to sections of single songs as if they're Legos or building blocks. Because I feel and take in music similarly, I can hear Tori Amos' songs like "Precious Things" and experience it in these same tangible sections. Excitement for each, the way they creep, crawl, and click into one larger piece to create a masterpiece.

I'm able to enjoy the way my friend's Jibneh (Syrian Cheese by Kasbo's Market) stretches long like the most delectable bubblegum. Only it's a nutty and salty storm in your mouth. And it's so good. Would this culinary experience be less if I wasn't sensory? I don't want to find out.

I don't drink alcohol more than once a month, so I drive my people around—I think my overresponse to stimuli might be why I don't like it. Alcohol kicks my senses into overdrive, and it's a disaster after 10 p.m. when you must wake up by 5 a.m. So, I can't always join in the celebrations the same way, but there are worse things than not enjoying an alcoholic beverage.

My children and I attended the show *Stomp* in Redbank. Because of my sensory stuff, the banging, the clanking, the patterns—I was sent into such satisfying territory, emotionally. *Stomp* is good for the senses to readjust. Loud concerts are highly encouraged for me as they take my sensory madness and place it back together in lightspeed segments. Outrunning my own brain.

The ceremony of Sharpie marker to paper in between novels and memoirs when I have writer's block ... then a fill in of watercolor or marker or crayon. All gifts being given to me from the way my nervous center operates.

My sensory stuff allows me to see the dichotomy of my hometown and the beauty that lives in the separate parts—as pure as the way certain streets and sections of the town smell and curve. Sidewalks dangled in honeysuckle, and alleys where diners keep their backdoor open for ventilation from the kitchen.

Understanding and adjusting is possible. It takes years sometimes, but again, maybe less now that there's more information and research about sensory defense.

Watching scenarios play out on film or TV give me anxiety if I get too immersed. I imagine their empty stomachs, their headaches, the smells. This is not ideal, but at least I know when to look away or not even bother with certain shows.

I do not want my sensory issues to disappear. They won't. In turn, I remain aware and prepared as best as possible. And I write the rest away using it as fuel for characters, settings, and mood, almost as if it's the creativity well that I swim in. Forever.

Acknowledgements

I always thank Kevin, Lenni, and Mallory because you are my favorites. Love you. I'd like to also thank Melanie Faith for your indestructible editing abilities and your encouragement that cannot be matched. Thank you, Jessica Bell and Amie McCracken, for your commitment to the publishing industry. Thank you, Ian and Suzanne, for being my best writing friends—your feedback, kindness, and comradery has been invaluable. Thank you to everyone who contributed to the "interruption" section—I won't name you, but you know who you are. Thank you, Benita and Corinne, for *all* the friendship on the daily. Thank you to the presses who published my work prior to this collection. Thank you, Mommy and Daddy, for the *best of times* on Mulberry Place.

Initial Publications of Essays:
"Mork" *Drunk Monkeys Press*
"Nectarine Pits" *Beach Badge* by Eight Stone Press
"Tickle My Arm" *Ovunque Siamo, New Italian-American Writing*
"The Texture of Voices" *elainawrites.com blog*
"Stars in My Mouth" *Beach Badge* by Eight Stone Press
"Billy's Tongue Made My Crotch Tingle" *Roi fainéant Press*

www.ingramcontent.com/pod-product-compliance
Ingram Content Group UK Ltd.
Pitfield, Milton Keynes, MK11 3LW, UK
UKHW012253290726
14090UKWH00016B/620

9 783988 321435